Coonhour

Coonhound Complete Owner's Manual

Coonhound care, costs, feeding, health, grooming and training all included.

by

Elliott Lang

Table of Contents

Table of Contents

Table of Contents

Acknowledgments

I would like to thank my friends and family for their unending support as I've composed this book. Special thanks goes to those friends and acquaintances of mine who claim ownership of dogs; their advice, experience and expertise made this publication better than it would have been otherwise.

Foreword

First of all I'd like to thank you for purchasing this guide to Coonhound ownership. It is with both pleasure and pride that I present it to you, the dog enthusiast. Its topics will both interest and inform prospective and current owners together with breeders. The book was created to address a perceived absence of a unified resource for those who own Coonhounds of any breed as a pet rather than as a hunting dog. Until now, those involved with the breeds have had to rely on magazines, spoken advice and bits and pieces of general knowledge and research. But no more!

Rather than being dry or difficult to read at length, I've endeavored to make this book readable, direct and plain-speaking whilst never compromising the purpose of informing the reader. As an owner of many dogs, I hope that the passion I've enjoyed in all my years spent with this wonderful animal is evident. Tailor making this guide to be accessible and even enjoyable has been a happy experience. My personal hope as a longtime lover of animals is that the information here serves to better the lives of many dogs and their owners.

I hope that you the reader can share in my enthusiasm and happiness as you tend to your Coonhound, and that this book will prove invaluable every step of the way.

Chapter 1. An Introduction To Coonhounds

The Coonhound is perhaps one of the most versatile and able scent hounds. The breed gained its name from one of its earliest jobs: hunting raccoon. Despite a legacy of hunting, this family of dogs have proven themselves to be wonderful in the home. Their desirable qualities and practicality as a companion in most larger sized residences make the Coonhound all too worthwhile an animal to consider for a pet.

This book intends to encompass questions owners both current and prospective might have regarding this dog as a pet. Some portions will work as a straightforward practical guide whilst others contain useful and specific knowledge to bear in mind. I've made sure to balance theory with practical advice. Coonhounds tend to provoke imagination in their owners. Don't be surprised if you make up a game or even invent a unique meal that your dog will love!

In this chapter we will refer to the Coonhound's nature as a strong scent and hunting hound in a historical context. It's true that whoever owns the dog as a pet will witness these characteristics emerging from time to time. Even the best trained dogs will let their instincts take over on occasion. For those keeping them as pets, owning both a short and long leash is vital.

Given the good nature and flexibility of all Coonhounds, a good attitude and regimen can see any of the half dozen breeds becoming wonderful, dependable and amiable home dogs with a decent lifespan. Affectionate but tending to calm restraint in the home, to me it does not seem outlandish to call the Coonhound underrated given its lovable nature and all-round strengths.

1) History

The Coonhound has a long and proud history. The initial breeds emerged during the early colonial days in the northern Americas. Colonists from Europe, wishing to farm, develop and tame the lands before them, realized that a hunting dog fit for purpose on the new lands would be required.

Using various existing breeds as a template, dozens of distinguished breeders became involved in creating a hound which fitted both the conditions of the fledgling colonies and of the rough, varied land which colonists so desired. Greater parcels of land cleared meant more food to support an ever-growing population. Farms already established suffered damage to crops from pest animals, frustrating those wishing for more than a foothold on the vast land before them. Initially the common fox was the prime target for the new breeds; only later could the dogs efficiently hunt native creatures such as raccoons.

Using the English Foxhound as a template, in the initial decades breeders experimented by crossing the best purebred foxhounds with other scent hounds. Occasionally gifted or extremely talented dogs would be discovered by hunters tackling the array of animals rendering the landscape a wild place. These rare specimens could be mixed into the gene pool on proving themselves, adding to the qualities desired.

Eventually by the end of the 1600s the first Coonhounds had emerged as a distinct breed capable of tackling the unusual challenges the new world held for those colonizing it. As the years went by, further Coonhounds were introduced. The colonies were showing their potential not simply as living space, but as lands plentiful in resources. On appreciating the successes of the new world, the first subsequent waves of European migration brought more of the old, established breeds of dog together with breeders both distinguished and capable.

It took hundreds of years for all six breeds of Coonhound to establish themselves as individually registered types of dog. Starting in the 19th century, many Coonhounds began to be appreciated as eager, happy pets at home. The hunting heritage which had defined their existence until that time began to diverge as well-off home owners began to appreciate the various breeds as companions and family members.

With increasing prosperity came an increasing number of people with the time and resources to devote to pets. By the 20th century the Coonhound was not simply an established scent hound in the United States, but had found a place in countries worldwide. Award shows, ownership by famous figures, as well as each breed's markedly different appearance and countenance saw each type of Coonhound attract a devoted following. As World War II came to a close, each breed was formally registered.

With the Coonhound counting amongst the most prominent of the scent hounds, its place as a dog of prominence worldwide is without doubt. Ownership across the world has only continued to rise as the Internet brings together enthusiasts. In an information age which sees so many knowledgeable and talking about all manner of dogs, the Coonhound's future is a bright one.

2) Breeds

By definition a breed is defined as a group of animals who've descended from a common ancestry. In tracing the lineage of a given dog, we can approximate not only when the hound's characteristics emerged, but also where certain qualities began to exemplify themselves. It's even possible to create dog family trees all the way back to a breed's beginning!

Coonhounds were initially bred to marry up an excellent sense of smell with a decent level of agility. The desire to create a new dog for new lands, in many ways cemented this group's destiny as a subset of purebred breeds distinct from any scent hounds that have come before or since. In the circumstances where a perceived aesthetic or practical improvement was made to the overall character, a new lineage was sometimes struck.

Most Coonhounds have a somewhat melancholy 'neutral' expression which can be mistaken for sadness to the untrained eye. This attribute, typical in the facial structure of many hounds, can be mistaken for genuine sadness by untrained eyes. Owners however attest to a variety of expression and emotive response that outstrips that of other hounds.

In the present day we are confronted by six different breeds of Coonhound who emerged distinctly in turn over centuries. With the exception of the Plott hound all are cousins of the others. Despite this, there is still some unique variation that isn't confined to appearances between the breeds.

Later on in the book we'll touch upon the general characteristics all Coonhounds share. First however let us profile each and every breed in preface to our looking in detail at the various makeup each dog brings to the table.

a) The American English Coonhound
Also known as the 'Redtick' Coonhound, this breed originally descends from English and American Foxhounds of antiquity. As such this breed is the oldest of all the Coonhounds. Centuries ago the early renditions of this hound tended to hunt foxes, which were a known pest to farmers in the new world. Brought to the American colonies during the 1600s, the breed was afterwards perfected by professional breeders and hunters as a dog well-suited to the terrain of the vast and untamed American continent. Animals new to the Europeans making inroads at the time, such as the raccoon and cougar, added to the calls for a breed explicitly suited for hunting such creatures.

Also known as the Redtick Coonhound, this dog is the forerunner and archetype of all but the Plott Coonhound. An athletic, fit and energetic hound, the American English Coonhound benefits from a scant need of grooming maintenance and a healthy constitution. The Redtick's intelligence and energy has proven advantageous through extended hunts. These qualities afford present-day owners convenience when training and caring for this dog.

As a dominant, profligate hound for over 200 years, breeders in the late 19th century were in a good position to split the genetic line into variants. We see today a vibrant range of colors between the breeds, which complements the relatively trim and fine build. American English Coonhounds remain popular, still being bred for both professional and domestic purposes.

b) Treeing Walker Coonhound

Originating from the Kentucky breeder John W. Walker, the Treeing Walker Coonhound was developed in the middle of the 18th century, using the finest stock of the famous "Virginia Hounds" as a basis on which to create a new breed. The dog's nature to instinctively chase animals up trees gives the breed name its verbal character.

A turning point for the fledgling breed came in the 19th century when a hunting hound stolen from Tennessee was introduced into the line. Noted for its brilliant hunting and running attributes, the hound was termed 'Tennessee Lead". This hound is to date the only authorized outcross the breed has received.

By the beginning of the 20th century the Treeing Walker hound was seen fit to be registered alongside the English Coonhound. Many diehard breeders of the Treeing Walker teamed together to request they be considered a separate breed, which they were in 1945.

Sharing the intelligence of their contemporaries, the Treeing Walker is a functional dog which enjoys activity. The coloration strongly resembles the common black/white/brown of the Beagle. However the elongated face and somewhat taller bearing set them apart from any other scent hound. As pets their ingrained 'hot nose', i.e. a tendency to hunt quickly and tenaciously, must be kept in check. On a walk the dog may run off to spontaneously hunt on their ("his" OR "its") own initiative!

c) Black and Tan Coonhound

Originating from the southern United States, the Black and Tan Coonhound's distinct appearance denotes the introduction of some Bloodhound stock to certain American Foxhounds during the 17th century. The Talbot hound, an ancient breed dating back to England at least 1000 years ago, was also introduced to the general stock which resulted in a separate breed towards the beginning of the 18th century. As such, the Black and Tan is thought of as the second established Coonhound.

Soon abundant in the American lands, by the end of the 18th century both Native American peoples as well as European colonists owned specimens which proved to be well-rounded in terms of ability, fitness and temperament. They have a notable musculature and stockiness compared to their lighter toned cousins. Those owning Black and Tans should thus be especially cautious on walks since the dog can dart away, seemingly forgetting the human on the other end of its leash!

With a distinct coloration to which it owes its name, at first glance the dog's physiology shares a resemblance both to the historic Bloodhound and its closer, Coonhound cousins. Other than the obvious differences in appearance, this breed distinguishes itself in the fact that it has a cold nose. This simply means that the hound can pick up and pursue trials formerly thought cold. As such you shouldn't be surprised if this dog suddenly strains against its leash on walks.

d) Bluetick Coonhound

A more recent addition to the Coonhound breed is the Bluetick which was developed in the Southern United States. Along with the variety of ancestors that form the modern Black & Tan Coonhound, the Bluetick also carries blood of certain French hounds which had long been used in seeking out big game.

The desired breed was produced once professionals had combined the steadfast size of the French hounds with the keynote agility and speed showcased by the already existing Coonhounds. Hunters wishing to achieve a compromise between speed and efficiency, and the desired 'cold nosed' qualities, were successful. Compared to other hunting hounds, the Bluetick is revered for its clear, strong voice which often helps trackers discern the exact actions and pursuits should the Bluetick be used for hunting.

Pet owners tend to value the Bluetick more for its unusual bluish spotted coat to which it owes its name. Cared for and given good grooming, a Bluetick can be quite striking to passersby.

The Bluetick had already emerged as a distinct breed by the end of the 19th century. For a time there was contention in how to categorize the dogs due to differences between the color of coats. Yet the breeding standards soon achieved consistency, and the Bluetick was duly separated from its redder cousins and classed as its own breed in 1945. Today, as with every kind of Coonhound, the Bluetick has its own hardcore breeding enthusiasts and groups devoted to it.

e)Redbone Coonhound

The singular, near-monotone coat of the Redbone Coonhound, together with its proud stature and bearing is what renders this dog the most showy of the Coonhound family. Tracing its ancestry back to the 1700s to the red Foxhound, this Coonhound became popular both in hunting and as an attractive pet during the industrial revolution.

Despite appearances, the Redbone hound has also been subject to vigorous breeding in the interests of good performance and receptiveness to instruction. Despite an incursion in the mid-19th century in which a subset of the breed had black 'saddlebacks', breeders strove for consistency. After over a century of this rigorous practice, the Redbone Coonhound as it is known today emerged. Given their attractiveness and bearing, the Redbone tends to be among the more expensive Coonhounds.

Possessing the robust constitution of its other cousins, the Redbone hound has become established as a popular pet at home. Several clubs and forums both online and off are devoted to a dog many find even-tempered and tolerant of a family atmosphere. If rigorously trained, a Redbone is quite capable of becoming a strong challenger in dog shows.

f) Plott Coonhound

Named for the distinguished breeder George Plott, the Plott Coonhound was established in America during the middle of the 18th century when a large set of Hanoverian hounds were introduced. Exclusively bred in the rugged, mountainous and cool climate of North Carolina, the Plott hound was created to aid in the hunting of bears.

Lithe, alert and nimble on the ground, the Plott is noted as one of the most intelligent of the Coonhounds. Unlike every other Coonhound, the Plott features no English foxhound ancestry, but has become classed as a noted hound within the USA given its prowess and ability in spite of difficult terrain. Despite the separation in lineage, the Plott hound still possesses a formidably loud baying bark.

Yet unlike any other Coonhound, the coat of the Plott hound varies greatly. Some can be solid black, others can be varying shades of brindled brown - brindle denoting a darker shade upon a lighter one. Markings can sometimes be vivid and attractive.

As a working dog the Plott hound is notably fearless and tenacious. It is perhaps underappreciated as a domesticated, family-friendly companion animal: mostly Plott hounds today are still bought and owned by those within the hunting scene. Despite the protective guarding by the descendents of George Plott, the hound is still not often found outside the Southern USA due to the family only selling the breed infrequently. Despite the difficulties to find a Plott to keep solely as a pet, a small coterie of owners has sprung up to speak in favor of the dog's gentle, intelligent character.

Chapter 2. Purchasing a Coonhound

If you've already narrowed your choice of dog to the Coonhound it likely means you have a strong idea of the quality of dog you'd like. Yet before you buy there are many questions you must ask yourself. First and foremost you should wonder just what you want a dog for - an excuse to get fit? A companion? A family member? Or a combination of these?

Having a breed in mind is great for focusing your search so long as their strengths and weaknesses are well-matched to the environment and lifestyle you can offer them. Coonhounds make tons of noise, need good diets, plenty of exercise, and plenty of discipline. In return you'll have a friend to be proud of for life.

Having mentioned your ambition to at least a few family members, you should think of your purchase as a long term commitment. A dog isn't a temporary gift or diversion, but is instead a living thing with needs that must be tended to day by day. Coonhounds, as with most scent hounds, will take over a large part of your life and best suit an active, lively family. In Chapter 3 we discuss negatives specific to the Coonhound breeds. You should also be mindful of the drawbacks of purebred hounds, which we'll cover extensively in that same chapter.

It's no lie that there are parallels between having a child and buying a puppy. Just as a child requires a fitting environment, nutrition, consistent cleanliness, hygiene plus care and attention so too does a puppy. In fact given how impressionable dogs are, it can be argued that as an owner you've more responsibility over a much shorter span of time. Simply put, you must be clued in to give your dog the best attitude and personality it is capable of having.

With these thoughts in mind, let's tackle the practical points you ought to consider as you set about acquiring a Coonhound puppy.

1) Locating A Reputable Coonhound Breeder

This phase of venturing to discover which dog you'd like is one of the most vital motions you'll make to dog ownership. Done considerately, you can end up owning a wonderful animal which ticks most, if not all, of the boxes. The commonest way to acquire a new Coonhound is to locate a breeder who deals specifically in scent hounds.

A breeder can be anyone from a dedicated professional who owns many kennels, to a family with a particular passion for one or two particular breeds which (or "that") take to advertising the occasional set of pups in the local newspaper.

A trait which some professional breeders showcase is in breeding for appearances. Some of these breeders-by-trade focus their breeding practices on their hounds competing in pet shows to win awards, whilst others do so merely out of a desire to prioritize style over substance. Given how this type of breeder values purity, the resulting dog can be inbred, of low intelligence, or angry.

Some online pet stores will offer to ship dogs to you, some even opting for a specialized transportation service. Given that your first meeting with your puppy and your use of intuition in the selection procedure is so vital, I do not recommend having a dog sent in the mail. As a living thing with character and emotion, a puppy would be the last thing I'd want to have travel a long distance.

As well as simply looking in your newspaper, there are a number of online directories listing details. More and more nowadays we see listed testimonials, verified reviews and (for professional breeders) personal websites. These can be very useful for narrowing down your search, but of course you shouldn't judge solely on appearances.

One more thing: despite how heartbreaking it might feel to leave, unless a given pup and breeder seem right to you, do keep up the search if part of you has doubts. It's always fine to go home, talk it through, check out another breeder or two before finally settling on a certain pup.

2) Examining The Puppy's Parents and the Litter

On arriving at the breeder's place you should first examine the parents of the litter or dog you'll be looking at. Most Coonhounds offered for sale tend to be purebred, so you'll be looking at two of the same breed when you conduct your examinations. Crossbred Coonhounds are rare, but do crop up from time to time.

Environment is a big consideration for Coonhounds. As a high maintenance dog, they need a large, free roaming environment to live in. Cages or small pens are certainly not suitable, although large playpen style constructions can be fine for when the dog is taking a rest. Always be watchful for signs of neglect. These can include notable slenderness wherein the ribs can be seen, or a poorly-kept coat.

A good breeder will certainly grant your wish to meet the parents. They may be kept separate or with the pups. You can ask to inspect each parent in turn should you wish. Does the setting fit the place in which the pups are kept? Given the climate and weather at the time, does it strike you that the dogs are properly catered for where they are?

Ideally both parents should display the typical qualities of well-roundedness: neither overbearing nor aggressive nor docile to the point of disinterest in you as a new person. They should be well fed, moderately gregarious, show signs of excitement and interest such as with a wagging tail or a casual, curious approach. If kept with the pups they should be caring, attentive and supervisory without being overly concerned.

Even Coonhound puppies emote very well. Happy, they'll make it known in a sustained and eager display. Sad, they might show some interest but will resume a somber passivity before long. It can be prudent to discreetly observe a litter's mood once you apparently lose interest in them. An uplifted, cheerful mood is the best in which you can ably spot the different personalities, which brings us to the next section.

3) What To Ask The Breeder

Ideally, you won't be the one doing most of the asking. Good breeders are keen, curious and probing with every prospective buyer. It might even feel like a job interview as they size up your commitment and passion. They might be spontaneous, giving you tips and ideas there and then, but almost any good breeder welcomes enthusiasm and questioning in turn.

Nevertheless it's great to have several ground rules to draw on as you converse and question. Firstly never be ashamed to ask something. When new to anything, including dogs, there are no stupid questions. A great first question is to ask the breeder what qualities they breed for. A breeder who wishes for good tempered dogs is often well-intentioned. Even if the breeder is an informal one, what you make of them as people is important if you wish to obtain a fine dog.

Before asking questions be sure to examine your own circumstances. Coonhounds are dogs bred for open areas and therefore tend to adapt poorly to apartment buildings or small houses without large yards. An exception might be if you live in a small house more or less adjacent to a park.

Contemplate too your location. Can you adopt a variety of interesting walking routes in the area? In any event, how much exercise do you desire to give your dog? Coonhounds need an hour's exercise daily. A top concern should be to provision it lest the dog become unhealthy and temperamental.

Consider the nature of those within your household, and the environment they desire. If you reside in a loud, bustling environment with one or more children, think about selecting a pup who'd fit in: an extroverted animal who enjoys stimulation and can both interact and tolerate people with ease. Alternatively if you'd like periods of quiet between the barking and activity, a more casual or submissive dog could be the way to go.

a) Medical Questions

Before you commit to purchasing a dog it's essential to cover the medical angle. Not only will questions regarding vaccinations cover every hound, a good breeder may have already registered each pup and kept a written, authorized record which they'll present you with on purchase. A simply phrased question such as "Have the pups had any vaccinations?" followed by "What additional vaccinations would you recommend?" should suffice.

You should also ask about the parents: have they had any outstanding health issues in life? Do they have or carry a risk of genetic defects? This can include orthopedic (bone) problems, a weak heart, or any number of ailments. Coonhounds as a rule tend not to have ingrained vulnerabilities, and congenital issues are very rare unless inbreeding is present.

You might also wish to ask about a recommended local vet with experience in dealing with Coonhounds. If further vaccinations or de-worming is necessary, you should know exactly where to go. A breeder confident about the dog's health will often suggest you get the puppy a general checkup, and agree to take back the pup should the vet conclude a malady of some kind is present.

Furthermore, inquiring about diet is usually a good move. Often breeders will have had good results with at least one prior generation, varying the nutrition with age. Though you needn't be so rigid what with intending your Coonhound as a pet, it can - especially in the months of puppyhood - be useful to emulate the breeder and take their recommendations seriously. Even casual home breeders can be attentive in this regard, even if it's just buying dog foods marketed at different ages.

b) Inquiring About Guarantees and Returns

Once you've settled on a particular breeder and what they offer, you should inquire about a potential guarantee and returns policy. Usually a returns guarantee for say 72 hours after purchase should be agreed upon. For whatever reason, you should be able to take the pup back within this short span of time.

A good breeder will stake their reputation upon a dog by drawing up a contract or promissory note which states that should any genetic defect emerge at any point in life the owner should be entitled to a refund to assist with vet bills. This should certainly apply with Coonhounds despite their generally robust health. Furthermore a contract should attest to the pup's already robust state of health and ability to pass a veterinary examination.

Certain breeders will also be open to accepting their pups back at any age in the interests of finding them a new home. Dedicated, professional breeders will include this in a contract. Should you be unable to care for the dog and cannot find a home, the breeder can promise to take the task on.

As such your questions should surround the exact specifications of a contract. The breeder should be upfront, open and not at all evasive as the terms are laid out. Examine what's written yourself before you commit to buy. There shouldn't be any verbose legalese; what's before you should be discernible and in plain English.

c) Testimonials

It's often a good idea to get a hold of other opinions where a breeder is concerned. As with other matters a good breeder will be open and upfront when it comes to honoring your request for some testimonials. Being able to talk with those giving the praise is great for information, especially if the past customer bought a pup from the same parents.

Often a large, established breeder will be proud to display feedback online. Smaller breeders might ask certain customers if they can provide an upfront testimony to the breeder's caliber over the phone or provision a written piece of feedback to be shown to future clients.

In any event it's helpful to inquire. The only possible exception would be if you choose to opt for a home breeder who only rarely sells any pups, whereupon you'd find it best to rely upon your own perceptions.

4) Temperament

If the puppies are at 8 weeks or older - the age at which they can be safely separated from their mother - often their personalities are becoming known already. If they're kept in a decent-sized pen or container, you should be able to tell the personalities apart readily. Does the Coonhound rise as you approach? Will it lick your hand when you offer it? Are some pushy, vying for attention over their siblings? Are they curious, sniffing about frantically?

An extroverted dog will often exhibit this sort of happy enthusiasm. In some litters they can even be the largest - an extroverted, forceful nature may also equate to a voracious appetite. Some Coonhounds, such as the Redbone and Treeing hound, are renowned fast eaters as it is. Though not a certain sign by any means, dominant, playful and extrovert dogs are as a rule demonstrative. At the other end of the scale we've the timid, unsure pup who often looks unsure of itself. Often the quiet, submissive dog will not mix, make noise or be playful, but will instead pursue affection with a simple look of dewy-eyed longing. Treated well, this type of dog gains confidence in itself so long as the affection of its owner is reinforced. Despite being less stimulated, this Coonhound's personality needn't be lazy: even a relatively subdued Coonhound should be exercised daily. It can sometimes be good to bring along a family member or two to observe the pups. The downside is that this can increase peer pressure before you've done a proper examination, but the upside is that family can fall in love and appeal to a pup's nature better than you ever could alone. Questions or simple observations can lead a breeder to elaborate on his views towards members of a given litter.

Sometimes a breeder will have the pups undergo a temperament test to gauge reactions. Things such as dropping an object nearby, cradling the puppy upside down whilst looking in his eyes or picking the dog up to test for struggling or objection can all indicate emerging temperament. Whilst not completely accurate, these tests often serve as at least a good indication and should be requested politely.7

5) Buying or Adopting an Adult Coonhound

Adult dogs can offer a fantastic opportunity for accustoming yourself with any given breed. Suitable adult hounds will tend towards an extroverted, eager personality so ruling out the possibility of separation anxiety.

Coonhounds generally tend to be flexible on being transferred to a different home. Intelligent and attentive, they are generally capable of taking to a new owner without much fuss so long as the environment and care is up to standard.

The training you'll give an adult dog differs very much from that which a puppy requires. Good adult hounds are housetrained, are well-socialized with those they meet and have settled into their personalities. They tend to be much less time consuming than puppies, who require time and love to mould into good dogs.

Other advantages include knowledge of a full health profile, a good idea of the dog's behavior and preferences regarding exercise, eating, and nature around people including children. Many people adopt an adult dog from a shelter, finding the adoptive process to be a moral duty to a perfectly good hound.

If you find you want to gain confidence and experience with Coonhounds, adopting an adult could prove the wisest decision. After a while and when your self-confidence has improved, you could proceed to considering a puppy. The topic of shelters will be visited in detail later in the book.

6) Suggestions By Country On Where to Buy

Listed below are suggested venues for research. I've included a few helpful online forums with large communities. Among other things, members can furnish you with advice and recommendations per your place of residence. These suggestions are particular to the Coonhound rather than being generalized dog enthusiast sites.

Also included are certain large breeding venues by geographic area of each country mentioned. Should you be willing to drive to the nearest city, please make sure to make preparations for the new pup in the car as per the travel advice later in this book. Phone numbers and contact e-mail addresses for the kennels are also noted where available.

a) USA & Canada

Given the heritage of the Coonhound in the US & Canada, there are dozens of websites dedicated to the breeds. Here's a selection of a few of the best among the blogs, forums, and informational websites around.

CoonDawgs is a large congregation of Coonhound owners. Not only do they include a huge list of suggested breeders, the large community present are mainly dedicated to the Coonhound as a hunting dog. Plenty of advice for pet owners is also present. Classified adverts are also present: http://www.coondawgs.com

Coonhound911 is the official webpage of the Michigan Coonhound Rescue. As well as serving as a center which places and foster Coonhounds, the website includes articles and information. An impressive photo gallery plus general information on dog adoption is also present. Those managing the site have spent over 20 years finding new homes for Coonhounds. If you wish to adopt an adult this can be a good place to start: http://www.coonhound911.org

American Black and Tan Coonhound Rescue concerns itself mostly with the titular breed. However there are occasionally other varieties on offer as well as Bloodhounds. The website maintains a location-indexed link and carries a application procedure: http://www.coonhoundrescue.com

In addition to these suggestions there are all sorts of localized breeder websites. Simply putting your state and town alongside 'Coonhound rescue/adoption/sale' within a search engine should be enough to turn some up for your consideration.

b) UK

Coonhounds are rare in the UK, although small numbers have started to be introduced over the past couple of decades. If you live in Britain and wish to acquire a Coonhound it will likely take research and time regardless of breed. I've included three websites that I've observed listing Coonhound puppies sold by breeders.

Pets 4 Homes maintains extensive information about Coonhounds, and occasionally has some on offer on the page. It is possible to have e-mail reminders, or contact the website in order to know as soon as possible when a Coonhound is on offer - http://www.pets4homes.co.uk

Our Dogs is a long running dogs magazine in the UK. The website includes frequently updated classifieds with Coonhound pups amongst other breeds. For full access, including contact with breeders present, it is possible to purchase a website edition trial membership of two months (£16 GBP) or a year (£65). https://www.ourdogs.co.uk

K9 Puppy offers a simple, functional search index which allows you to search a database of current listings. You can narrow your search to individual breeds of Coonhound. Note that some breeds, such as the Bluetick and Plott hound, are not present: http://www.k9puppy.co.uk

c) Australia & New Zealand

As is the case in Britain, Coonhounds in Australia are scarce but carry a small and devoted following. Occasionally some breeds, particularly Blueticks and Black and Tans, will appear for sale. Back in the 1990s a small hardcore of breeders was responsible for the Bluetick's official recognition as a breed in Australia. The Black and Tan was recognized in 2009, and there is some enthusiasm for gaining its acceptance in Australia too.

The Australian Dog Forum is a large community of dog owners and breeders. Given the rarity of any Coonhound in Australia or New Zealand, discussion is uncommon but polite requests are always welcome. http://www.australiandogforum.net

Dogz Online is a large group of purebred dog enthusiasts. As well as records of dog shows and classifieds there's a useful forum too. Occasionally news of Coonhounds becoming available passes by these sites. The Australian version is located here - https://www.dogzonline.com.au

The New Zealand version is located here - https://www.dogzonline.co.nz

Bassets deals not only with Basset hounds, but with Black and Tan Coonhounds too. The kennels are based in Waikato, New Zealand. The website includes galleries and a contact page to request updates on the newest litters available. http://www.bassets.co.n z

As well as these, there are numerous websites with an indexed search. Coonhounds are listed on several of these, but are infrequently seen. I recommend holding discussions online to aid your investigation. The enthusiasm shown in your initiative may serve to get you the Coonhound pup you've so wanted.

7) Puppy and Adult Pricing

Breeder prices vary between breed and location. In areas where Coonhounds are scarce, the prices can be far higher. Large breeders tend towards a rigid pricing structure and tend not to allow haggling. Smaller or home breeders can sometimes be negotiated with.

If a purebred puppy has documentation proving its lineage this can often increase the price. Crossbreeds or dogs without documentation tend to be cheaper. Despite the higher cost, purebred Coonhounds do have the advantage of a community of informed and dedicated breeders.

The estimates below are intended as a rough guide only.

Redbone Coonhound

Typically $400 - $700 for a puppy.

Approx. $300 - $500 for an adult.

Bluetick Coonhound

Typically $150 - $400 for a puppy.

Approx. $150 - $350 for an adult.

Black & Tan Coonhound

Typically $350 - $600 for a puppy.

Approx. $250 - $500 for an adult.

American English Coonhound

Typically $200 - $400 for a puppy.

Approx. $200 - $350 for an adult.

Treeing Walker Coonhound

Typically $150 - $300 for a puppy.

Approx. $150 - $250 for an adult.

Plott Coonhound

Typically $300 - $500 for a puppy.

Approx. $300 - $400 for an adult.

8) Purchasing Ethically

One pitfall even seasoned purchasers of dogs can fall into is falling prey to those who run a 'puppy mill'. A growing issue worldwide, it is estimated that millions of puppies are sold through such places each year. Although no established, precise definition exists, puppy mills essentially refer to breeding which is about making money over a direct concern for the given animal's welfare. Puppy mills aren't limited to any breed. A dog's first weeks or months spent in such a place can lead to all manner of behavioral, social and physical health issues along the line.

Separating sound breeding practices from unethical ones can be accomplished by following the discernment methods outlined in the above sections. A puppy mill owner is less likely to hold a sincere, obvious passion for their dogs and will not bother to question you much regarding your home life, attitude and motivations behind wanting a new dog. Environment can be very telling too: the sort of breeder who locks both mother and father in dirty cages using a production line philosophy is not the kind of person capable of showing true feeling and passion for animals. A reluctance to show you around the premises should be considered suspicious.

Good breeders will never separate the puppies from their parents until they're at least six weeks old. This period of weaning is vital for the puppy's ability to survive and thrive. Despite how cute infant pups look, bear in mind that those who are very young should not even be on display. The pups you do buy should be at least somewhat older, well-fed, and enthusiastic.

Bear in mind that an absence of things we've covered, such as a reasonable returns policy, provision of medical and vaccination history, willingness to show you the parents, the conditions of the breeding ground and a ready ability to provide testimonials are all indicators of a mill-type venue or at least a subpar standard of quality.

Chapter 3. The Right Choice of Dog

We've already mentioned differing personalities of dogs and your need to be aware of circumstances at home during the selection process. Despite their history as hunting dogs, Coonhounds can adapt well to homes so long as you can tolerate their shortcomings.

Every dog has flaws. Before buying it's important that you discover and discuss these negatives with those in proximity. There's nothing worse than acquiring a new dog then having to return it when you find it just isn't working for you or others. Coonhounds, given their intelligence and sensitivity, can mature into excellent pets given dedication. It's no secret that scent hounds are time consuming, demanding and a lot of work.

By the end of this chapter I'd like you to be certain that you're capable, have the approval of those around you, and have the time, energy and motivation to take on a challenging and engaging breed like the Coonhound. There really aren't half measures with dogs. There will be moments of frustration or impatience, you will be investing hundreds of hours in training, socializing, exercising, feeding and playing, and - provided you can handle the pressure - you will come out at the other side with a loving, well-adjusted dog you can be proud of.

Coonhounds are commonly billed as a hound for those with experience. Whilst a honed knack for dogs isn't essential, it is at least recommended that you're committed, have done your reading and have, at minimum, spent some time handling and getting to know dogs at certain points in the past. Although it's healthy to want a challenge, it's also sensible to be realistic about your abilities as a dog person.

1) Before Buying - Weighing the Pros and Cons

The first ground rule with this dog is that they really shouldn't be left unaccompanied during the day. You cannot depart the house to do shift work or run lengthy errands without leaving somebody at home to care, feed and watch over them. Tolerant, forgiving neighbors are a must: even a happy Coonhound can, in its joy, bark and bark and bark some more. Despite this, their repertoire of sounds varies, which to some dog lovers can be endearing.

Though not haughty or choosy by any means, the Coonhounds are limited to certain arrangements in residency. If you live in a city, a park must be within close distance of your house. The house itself must be a decent size with a fair amount of roaming space. A reasonably large garden is also an advantage.

Depending on your own preferences, a minimum of an hour spent exercising your dog through walks and play can be either a good or bad thing. The Coonhound will not settle for less without finding its own outlets for energy. They are by nature an energetic, enthusiastic dog. Indulging this vital instinct will go a long way to earning the dog's lasting respect and love.

With these requirements out of the way, let's proceed to the general pros and cons behind the Coonhound.

a) Good Things About Coonhounds

Coonhounds adapt to family life extremely well. Their amiable nature, whilst not necessarily easy going, makes them a good choice if you have children. Despite their innate social breeding, it is wise to keep smaller children, under supervision when the dog is around.

The Coonhound was bred to work with other dogs, sometimes in packs of ten or more. This lineage means that they tend to mix very well with all kinds of dogs, whether they be strangers encountered on walks or other dogs in your family. For stranger dogs, some socialization training will likely be needed to prevent undue reaction.

Despite their intelligence, Coonhounds tend to reject some conventional training. However this can be turned into an advantage given that every breed is very motivated by dog treats and certain snack foods as reward. When contented, they will simply tend to lay at your feet, accepting a lot of petting and affectionate scratching.

Putting aside the tough, alert and strong appearance, the Coonhound tends to strike a fine balance between emotional sensitivity and an outgoing, spontaneous, lively nature. If you want to preserve this happy balance, do however expect to deal with bursts of sudden energy which must be released by exercising the dog.

Their short coats need only infrequent washing and, given their manageable size and temperament, grooming tends to be neither too frequent nor overlong. A great advantage is the ease with which you can tell the Coonhound's mood: the features, posture, and poise are very explicit. You'll easily learn your dog's reactions, likes and dislikes by just looking at them.

Aside from relatively minor concerns such as infections of their large, floppy ears, the Coonhound is famous for a lasting health and steady constitution. Bred to cope for extended times on large frontiers often lacking in medical provision, the Coonhound has no susceptibilities provided it enjoys a standard of care throughout its life and especially in youth.

b) Bad Things About Coonhounds

When restless or bored, Coonhounds can lose all abandon and set about acquiring some very bad habits: tearing up chairs and sofas, voraciously digging up your garden, sounding off for the sake of it, thereby angering neighbors and even escaping your premises if they're able. This is a smart, even wily dog. They have been known to silently observe owners opening gates and then to do so themselves. Noise is often a big issue - a single Coonhound can produce a deep, loud bark which you ought to bear in mind.

Being bred for cooperation and sociability has its downsides. The Coonhound must have either a companion dog or person present almost constantly. Left solitary for more than a couple of hours, they can start to scratch or chew all manner of things even if you fulfill their needs for exertion! Even if you have other, less vigorous dogs, the ebullient charisma the Coonhound has, often encourages those dogs to join in with any mischief.

Unless they have grown up with other animals which you've perhaps had play with them, such as cats, the Coonhound can be tenacious or even dangerous. They should not be walked without a leash, which can be lengthy if you're in an area free of smaller creatures. Even if you do a fantastic job with training, expect the dog to catch and bring you rodents or even, occasionally, larger pests should you use a long leash with them in certain places.

Despite their physical prowess and boundless ability, Coonhounds can be deeply sensitive. A simple scolding can render them sulky and miserable. They end up laying upon the floor looking doleful, despite bounding around enthusiastically mere minutes earlier. As such, the Coonhound must be treated attentively, scolded firmly but carefully and trained to know when you're displeased with their conduct. Despite being fantastic at sensing things, Coonhounds aren't psychic.

2) One? Or More Than One?

It can be tempting as you browse a litter to take more than one of the super cute little pups home. Small as they might be, it's best to refrain unless you're absolutely sure you can keep them all their lives. This isn't renting: dog ownership is a lifetime commitment in all senses: financial, emotional and physical.

Coonhounds tend to bond well with most any breed of dog and enjoy keeping each other company. They were bred to have a deep, fraternal bond with others in a pack. This also means they can behave as they might on a hunt when you're walking them. Handling two full-grown Coonhounds straining at their leashes is a test of strength; managing three or more is a considerable achievement.

Should you already own cats or one or more small dogs it might be wise to pause before purchasing multiple Coonhounds. Whilst a single well-behaved, well-trained Coonhound can refrain from overenthusiastic play, several can gang up on those which are especially small, with potentially hurtful consequences. Although Coonhounds are as a rule affable and well-behaved, you must be confident and watchful should you decide to take on two or more in such a household. Intensive training to curtail bad behavior and play with other creatures can be done, but means additional time and commitment.

Caring for multiple Coonhounds is definitely not for beginners. Whilst one can be properly raised with guidance, two can be a handful even for a well-honed pet owner. Unless you're comfortable with your abilities and those of the people you live with, I recommend refraining from getting two, three or more dogs.

3) Male or Female?

Both genders of Coonhound are very similar in habit and overall nature. Neither is different in terms of aggression, although a bitch (female) will defend her newborn pups should she feel threatened or intimidated. This behavior is common amongst dogs of any kind.

Males tend to be somewhat larger than bitches both in terms of size and weight. However the size difference isn't overly significant; a few inches and perhaps 10 to 20 lbs sets the sexes apart. In Chapter 13 we'll cover these specifications in detail.

If you already have some male dogs within your household, it might be favorable to buy a male Coonhound so as to avoid unwanted pregnancies. Spaying can take care of this issue, although it can also affect temperament as we'll discuss later.

Coonhounds of either gender can be great pets, meaning gender shouldn't be high on your priorities as you select your new dog.

4) Age Concerns

The age of those around you must be considered as you make your choice of dog. Children should be old enough to be considerate and well-behaved around the Coonhound. As a rule Coonhounds mix well with children and will never be violent or fierce with them. However, excess noise or misbehavior can unsettle or cause upset.

Consider any elderly people living with you or nearby concerning possible sensitivities to noise. Be sure to consult them first. Play a video of a Coonhound to see how people find the noise. Given that older people tend to sleep lighter, the barks and bawls of a Coonhound might act to disrupt sleeping patterns.

Having someone around who is young and strong enough to handle the dog on a walk when you happen to be busy or absent from the home is important. A committed 'pet sitting' friend or relative can fill what can be a vital function for your Coonhound. Just remember that strength is a factor when exercising the dog.

5) Making Preparations At Home

Prior to the puppy's arrival, a few purchases and ground rules should be laid out. Things needed include food and water bowls and a few small toys. These and a simple bedding arrangement should be fine for the initial days. Other essentials can be thought about once the pup has settled, for instance grooming equipment, a collar and leash and a spray to remove bad smells.

The pup's bed within the house needn't be elaborate, but should be comfortable: simple, easy to wash cotton bedding in a big box. Your dog should have a little area of its own, at least a portion of a room in which he can sit, relax and enjoy some solitary time.

An often neglected principle is to settle on your very first commands, so the puppy isn't confused. If necessary, pin a list to the refrigerator, so that everyone in the house can memorize them in the weeks prior to the pup's arrival. If you wish to delegate tasks between those in the household, now would be the time to settle on a regular routine that fits everyone's personal schedule. Likewise, the basics of proper play and treatment should be made clear to everyone at home.

Safety concerns also merit looking at. Any sharp or dangerous objects should be kept out of reach. If you keep any stores of food close to the ground make sure they are either locked away in a pantry or elevated. Exposed wiring should be removed, medicines, cleaning chemicals and bleaches should be put out of any conceivable reach of the puppy.

Prior to the dog's training, it's very prudent to apply plastic coverings to wooden or fabric furnishings. Even a puppy can, in moments of bored caprice, take to scratching at things it shouldn't. The same goes for fragile objects. If you've a plant in the hallway atop a little stand, consider moving it to a windowsill. If you've a vase or other decorative items in places the puppy may be bounding through, move them.

Doormats can be kept in place but if you've expensive rugs, it is best to roll them up until the puppy has been properly trained not to claw and bite.

The First Days and Weeks With Your New Pup

The journey home should be one which both stimulates and acclimatizes the puppy. Whether you're one mile or fifty miles from the breeder, it will be an exciting time for the puppy who is all too likely to look around, enraptured and curious about all the passing sights.

On the ride home, scent hounds should be kept in a thick cardboard crate-type box which is small enough for the puppy to look out of. Thickness is important since the pup may take to scratching it, if only to enjoy the sensation the material confers. Scent hounds like the Coonhound may be excited with all the new odors, encouraging such behavior further.

Before you leave, the breeder will likely brief you on dietary matters. They will outline what the puppy has been fed and what you should transition into over the next few months. It's important that you match the puppy's existing diet prior to introducing or phasing out aspects. At such an early stage in life, gastric conditions such as diarrhea or general nausea can be a threat to the animal's health and growth. After the initial stages of ownership you can introduce variety to your dog's sustenance, making meals enjoyable.

Once the puppy is home, make sure you introduce the pup to the various portions of your home. Principally you should showcase the area you'd like to be the toilet, before moving on to the places where you would like the pup to feed, play and relax. Get the dog used to the layout of your home and allow for some autonomy as the day goes by.

Routine is perhaps the most important thing to settle upon in the first few weeks. It isn't so much about strict timekeeping: most dogs tend towards flexibility, especially once they realize a house can be full of activity at certain times. With Coonhounds the exception to this will be exercise which must happen at a certain time each day. In the formative few weeks, however, simple yard freedom suffices for the young hound.

Make sure that both the dog and those delegated to its care keep up with their respective duties. Ideally you should give the dog a name within a week of its arrival. As you work your way through the weeks, gradually adopt differing tones for discipline, beckoning, praise and so on. Dogs have excellent hearing, and discern tone as well as words when around those who care for them.

6) Common Mistakes New Owners Make

Making mistakes is one of the best ways to learn. However it's important that you recognize where you've gone wrong and correct yourself. Neglecting to do so could mean your puppy grows up with bad habits.

The mistakes listed below cover your own behaviors towards a new puppy.

a) Letting A Puppy Sleep On Your Bed

Allowing a puppy to sleep on your bed can have the puppy feel a sense of entitlement in the long term. Although it might be tempting when the dog is small and cute, remember that before long your Coonhound will grow. This is one example where too much love can be a disadvantage.

Although shed fur isn't too much of a concern with Coonhounds, the dog's presence at night can still be aggravating for those with allergies or asthma. Couple this to the fact that your dog can have dreams and wake up in the middle of the night, scratching with claws or kicking with his legs.

Sometimes this situation is okay with smaller dogs. However Coonhounds are, without exception, large hounds. Sensitive to sound and excitable, keeping them in bed isn't sensible. You might think a compromise would be to keep him there during the puppy months, moving him to his own bed or crate at a later date. Sadly the dog will find departing hard, and may behave badly. Training your dog out of this behavior is neither fun nor a worthwhile way to use your time.

b) Excessive or Strenuous Play

Overenthusiastic play when the dog is young can lead the dog to conclude that it's acceptable to behave that way much of the time. This goes for times when guests arrive, or at inappropriate times such as early or late in the day. Training can also become more difficult if your dog is jumping about and heedless to discipline.

If you've picked a dog with a high temperament, as is the case with many Coonhounds, you should practice restraint during play so as to not let overactive behavior become the norm as the puppy advances to adulthood.

c) Hand Play

Playing with your hands can be tempting with a puppy. They seem cute, harmless and fun especially when you use your hands to play with them. Since all dogs consider you another dog, including puppies, they'll tend to play with you as they would other dogs. Unfortunately their baby teeth are sharp and can easily pierce your skin. Allowing this roughness to continue with you, the master, signals approval to the young pup to continue being rough with his mouth.

The total absence of your hands shouldn't be the goal. Instead you should let out a yelp of your own as he bites. After he stops turn away and stop playing altogether. This sends a message and replicates the behavior a pack would exhibit. After a few times your puppy will get the message that biting is bad, and will memorize that for the future.

d) Poor Schedule and Discipline

A common error which is especially damaging for Coonhounds is the lack of schedule and discipline present in your puppy's life. There are times where your pup can simply roam around and do as he will, within reason. You should keep to a pre-written, pre-discussed schedule of training, feeding and exercise. Bedtime and waking time are important too.

There must be a certain amount of self-discipline in enforcing these things. Find a happy balance which keeps your dog contented; neither pampered nor neglected. Steadily increase your dog's exercise schedule and play regime, but slowly. These formative months are a balancing act; the reward at the end of the puppy 'tightrope' being a dog you love and are proud of.

7) Starting To Bond With Your Coonhound

You've lived together for a few weeks, and should by now have gained your puppy's trust. It's likely the dog looks up at you expectantly, consistently wags its tail on your arrival, and is starting to learn how to behave.

Your Coonhound doesn't just bond to you, it also bonds to the home environment. Having the basics such as toys is vital. A crate - contrary to myths about such devices being cruel confinement - appeals to your dog's primal instinct of making dens. A crate with bedding and a water bowl that's always full can really make your dog warm to you and the regime you set.

As the weeks pass you'll likely discover certain likes and dislikes your Coonhound carries: scratching behind the ears, rubbing the belly, or even letting him sit across your knees. A good time to indulge in such affection is evening, curled up in a warm place watching TV or reading. Allowing your puppy a chance to enjoy your leisure time with you is great for the bonding process. A relaxing evening sitting in the quiet can promote a silent affection which acts to compliment the commands and noise of daytime.

Other people and animals are a part of this too, and their acceptance of your new dog is just as important as yours. There should not be a rivalry between animals and everyone in the house should treat the dog with kindness.

After a few weeks, your dog will identify your house as home. Although training should have already begun at this point, an acceptance of the environment and those sharing it will only aid in your Coonhound's physical and personal growth.

Chapter 4. Types and Colors of Coats

1) Types of Coat

The difference between Coonhound coats is strictly down to breed. In terms of consistency and length of coat hair, every breed of Coonhound is similar. As a rule Coonhounds universally share short, smooth and often shiny coats which are lauded for their ease of grooming.

A true distinction can be made when we examine the dog at different ages. The Coonhound puppy's coloration is obtained very early in life, with the patterning often distinct once the dog reaches two months in age. This precocious emergence allows those breeding the hounds for shows to select and concentrate upon certain puppies from a young age.

For instance when we examine the American English Coonhound, a large amount of black is considered undesirable. Usually that breed will keep an even, lively patterning of three colors; a so-called 'tricolor hound'.

The quality of ticking is one which some Coonhounds are noted for. The word refers to patterns of small colored spots only visible on whiter parts of a dog's coat. The density of ticking varies from dog to dog, but in some Coonhounds it is so intense that the breed name is influenced, as with the Redtick and Bluetick.

Although ticking does occur with the dark colored dogs, it's invisible. As such the quality can only be discerned in American English (aka Redtick), Bluetick and Treeing Walker hounds.

The Treeing Walker is known to be quite heavy in shedding its fur compared to other Coonhounds. If you or anyone in the home are sensitive or allergic to dog fur, it would be wise to take this into account.

2) As A Puppy

A defining aspect of all Coonhounds is that their coloration is evident even from a very young age. In the breeds light enough to evidence it, ticking will also show up even a couple of weeks after birth.

A great thing about inspecting puppies is that the colors and their patterns will almost always be preserved into adulthood. The common dots of brown above each eye of the Black & Ta, not only look attractive but inform you as to whether the proper breeding is present.

There is no temporary coat that is shed towards adulthood. Rather we've a puppy who gives a good idea of his lifelong appearance. If you want to prioritize the appearance of your Coonhound, you can safely pick a pup knowing it will mature with the distinct markings continually present.

3) As An Adult

When your Coonhound reaches maturity, the patterning which was first distinguished during youth is now complete. You should be able to observe how the patterns have expanded: roughly, but not exactly, in line with what you'd expect from observing the dog's coat as a pup.

Since a Coonhound's coat is dictated as much by nutrition as it is by good grooming, the overall shine and quality will vary. It's important to take care with your dog whilst on walks or even in the garden: the rough and tumble nature of a Coonhound can mean scars may be picked up. This is another reason fighting tendencies must be curtailed early in life. Given the shortness of the coat the damaged tissue can be evident. It's wise to keep a leash on your Coonhound so as to prevent roaming through rough terrain.

4) Colors By Breed

Below is a description of each breed's typical coloration. The coats may shine to the point of carrying a varnished appearance if the Coonhound enjoys regular grooming and a good diet.

English American Coonhounds tend to be either white and brown or white, brown and black. A distinctive black ticking can be present in some varieties.

Bluetick Coonhounds are named for the bluish ticking which tends to cover their bodies and legs. The head is often black and the muzzle commonly white. Spots of tan can be present on the head.

Redbone Coonhounds gained their name for their singular reddish-brown or deep brown coat. Sometimes the belly, the area around the forelegs and bits of the head can be white.

Treeing Walker Coonhounds often carry a tricolor coat. The back is often colored black whilst the neck, legs and tail tend to be a deep white. The ears, upper face around the eyes and the hind quarters, are commonly a rich brown which can vary in tone due to breeding.

Black & Tan Coonhounds are, as you'd expect, black and tan in color. Of all Coonhounds this is the most uniform. A body entirely black, except for the feet, muzzle and sometimes the tops of both the hind and forelegs, carrying a single shade of brownish tan. A spot of tan above each eye is a keynote feature.

Plott Hounds vary most. Some Plotts are completely black without a trace of differing coloration. Others can be greyish with specks of dark ticking. Commonly, however, they carry a basic brown coat with patches and ticking of a darker shade lending a distinct look.

Chapter 5. Training

Training Coonhounds is as rewarding as it is enigmatic. As with most things Coonhound however, it does require kindness, patience and novelty. Many Coonhounds reject conventional methods unless motivated by treats. This tendency leads many owners to resign themselves to keeping the dog poorly disciplined. At worst, the bad habits and unruliness a bad training regime leads to can lead owners to contemplate taking the Coonhound to a shelter.

The modern manner of training began two generations ago. Until then trainers would behave starkly and violently compared to how they do in the 21st century. In the old days, pain was seen as a good motivator for even the youngest of dogs. It was, for instance, seen as perfectly acceptable to use collars and leashes to drag along a reluctant hound, essentially choking the dog until it obeyed.

Naturally this had negative long term effects on most dogs' temperaments. Sudden moments of unwarranted aggression, health problems leading to expense and a shortened lifespan, plus bad interactions with other animals were among the many consequences of training as it was in times gone by.

Nowadays, however, training aims to be humane, constructive and positive. Discipline is taught not through pain but through incentive; the carrot being far commoner than the stick. As well as simple affection through petting and compliments, we've use of treats and even toys as a means of motivating a dog towards competency.

A trained dog is a joy to behold: with no bad habits, consistent obedience, and no bothersome behaviors such as rudeness to guests. He won't leap up on you, rather he'll accept affection and ask for it in a discreet, respectable way. Methods of training vary; given the stubborn nature of Coonhounds it can be favorable to alternate between methods in order to obtain the best results.

1) The Basics

What should you teach your Coonhound first? There are a few select commands that begin your dog's education. The end goal of knowing the commands listed below, is the dog being able to obey these commands most of the time after one utterance.

Sit is likely the most well-known command associated with dogs. This command will prevent the bad habit of jumping, and will have the dog stop rather than run ahead of you when you're opening doors. If misbehavior occurs, the command, said sternly, can act to make the Coonhound desist quickly.

Lie down, or go lie down, acts to send the dog to another place when you don't want him around. If your dog is bothering you when you're busy doing chores or tasks, or during meals, or pestering others, this utterance can have him retreat to his bed or to an area you designate.

Easy is perhaps the hardest of basic commands to teach your Coonhound. Designed to give the dog cause to slow down or stop straining at a leash during walks, asking your dog to take it easy is good at keeping a pace manageable. In the Coonhound's case it may well prevent the dog from straining your arm.

Come, or alternatively come here, is more or less the opposite of lie down. Beckoning your dog to approach to eat, to commence exercise, or just to relax of an evening is an important thing. Whilst simply calling the dog's name can serve the same purpose, since you'll be making that sound in other contexts, it can be confusing for the dog.

Stay can be used if you want your dog to remain stationary. This can be useful when you want to attach a leash, keep the dog still during grooming, or when you need to bring (? "fetch" OR "get") something. This is a command where physical distance and time matters, with a sure sign of progression being the dog remaining still even when you're out of sight and, later, out of the hound's hearing range.

2) **Human Training**

It's undeniable that in training your dog, you must train yourself. Reading and assimilating knowledge is only part of the job. Be aware that your dog can be just as coercive in getting you to do things he finds beneficial but which might be considered unpleasant or annoying in the long run. Manner with guests and begging at the table can eventually mean your Coonhound is excluded from much of family life.

For such an intelligent and engagingly social dog as the Coonhound this can lead to more misbehavior and poor habits. If you put the Coonhound outside for being naughty inside, and it starts to bark and howl very loudly, what can you do then?

You should ask yourself and your family what the limits should be. Can you tolerate or even enjoy feeding at the table? Would you play during the evening when you find the dog drops a toy or ball on you? Importantly, do you think you can trust your Coonhound to go off-leash on certain walks?

All of these questions are important. Coonhounds are sensitive and only want to bond with their owners any way they can. Working out a compromise that fits your principles and the emotional, physical and nutritional needs of the dog in an environment is part of your training as a human being.

You should divorce yourself from human concepts of morality. A dog does not feel dutiful through a sense of integrity, but is instead deeply concerned with his own welfare. This simple sort of selfishness is what you need to mould. As such, deterrents and punishment won't work if you externalize human behaviors.

Projecting human traits upon the dog is a common pitfall during training. It's a lame excuse to term a dog too stubborn or stupid during training, or believe your dog acts out of a covert malice. The mentality you should keep is that your dog will obey and be faithful strictly because he wants something, is having fun, and through proper, sensitive training. From catering to this, all the positives of owning a dog emerge - in other words your own reward.

3) Learning Your Dog's Manner

A great way to proceed through training is to emulate your dog in being watchful. As you introduce new environments observe how your dog behaves. As with most routine tasks, it's a matter of trial and error as well as being sensitive. Once accomplished at reading your dog's emotions you can make the right responses. At the end of the process you'll have a good sense of noticing your dog's manner and can give commands and steadily add new ones accordingly.

A good thing to remember is that your dog cannot experience guilt. If he behaves wrongly, say by stealing and gobbling down some food left within his reach, it's useless to punish him afterwards. He cannot associate such punishment with what he did, even though he might remember how tasty that food was. Thus the look your dog gives popularly associated with guilt is instead one of anxiety and sadness once you've shown your anger.

Coonhounds as a rule are hard to train. Their sense of smell means that if you do leave food out, it will at least attract the dog. In a positive sense however, you could attempt discipline by setting the situation up and 'catching' the dog in the act. So long as you intervene during the attempt, your Coonhound should soon learn it shouldn't make such attempts once scolded.

4) On To Training

The oldest forms of training were pioneered about a century ago, and put into wide practice in the decades after World War II. The structure essentially surrounds combining recognition of good behavior with commands and signals to that end. Coaching consistency meets the goal which is a well-behaved Coonhound acting as you would like it to.

Corrections refer to something done to avert the dog from bad behavior, as or immediately before the act takes place. Timing is crucial. This can be anything from uttering the dog's name in a cutting way, looking and posturing threateningly, or throwing something that won't cause harm at the dog.

Such corrections must be varied. Some bold dogs won't respond to posture, whilst quiet, timid ones may get upset at being loudly scolded. Coonhounds have the added difficulty of behaving inconsistently with their general personalities. Despite tough exteriors, even extroverts can crumble to misery on what you might think of as a moderate correction. Thus, experimentation is essential.

Conditioning

The well-known tale of Pavlov's dogs embodies the essence of this kind of training. Use of a bell or even a buzzer will signify something is about to take place. In Pavlov's case this was feeding: he'd feed his dogs shortly after ringing a bell. After a time, the dogs would salivate even when no food was present - the dog had learned to associate a bell with food.

People inadvertently do this all the time. Chopping vegetables, opening and closing drawers, even turning on the gas stove can have a dog perk up knowing feeding time is near. Whistling often replaces 'come here' and so on. As such this method can be used alongside others to reinforce or least grant a backup to what you're already teaching.

In the case of the Coonhound, this training can be particularly successful. Sensitive to noise, the dog can come to recognize and obey distinct sounds especially if you incorporate them into feeding time. A thing to bear in mind, however, is to keep the noise moderate, as it may end up rendering your Coonhound overexcited.

Marrying up these methods with positive and negative reinforcements - i.e. treats, praise, petting and affection for good behavior whilst bad behavior merits scolding, angry looks and posture, and a thrown toy.

Once your Coonhound accepts consequences, he'll behave in an all-round receptive way. You can continually add more commands and start to introduce signals. Marrying up sight is far harder however, so it may be wise to try signals once your dog has already accomplished the basics.

5) Rules Of The Game

One of the central principles of training is to be firm but gentle in encouragement. Remember that harsh scolding for something that's already happened, from a loud spell of barking at night to excreting indoors, to chasing cats isn't constructive. Interrupting or immediate reactions really are the only way you'll have success - otherwise whatever you do will be misinterpreted.

Repetition is a fact of life with dogs. Even well-trained Coonhounds will need a command repeating at times. Given the Coonhound's vastly better hearing, you need only speak commands in a normal voice which isn't loud or forceful. Make sure you utter the dog's name prior to each command, as this will encourage attention.

Remember that dogs were designed to live in a hierarchical structure. Alpha wolves would be in charge of a pack, leading hunts, taking the choice cuts of meat, the choice females with which to mate, and would act to defend the pack should rivals or other threats arrive.

Whilst your position as a dog owner is far removed from the role of an alpha wolf, some aspects of leadership remain, particularly if you reside in multi-dog homes. Simply put, you must take charge regardless of how you view your dog. Given the complicated nature of modern life, you must be the one calling the shots.

This rule is important with training. A benevolent leader will seek to control a dog's mobility and movements, which is much of what training is in a nutshell. Once your dog knows this, you can with confidence progress to more and more training and commands.

6) Sit!

With your Coonhound on the floor, place your right hand against his chest and your left atop his shoulders. Then, run your left hand over his back down to the knees, applying equal pressure with both hands. Remain silent as you make this motion.

With your Coonhound now in a sitting position, mentally count to five before offering praise. After he's heard this, release him.

Primarily mastering the sitting command is like teaching your dog better manners for greeting someone. Although it's great to see your dog jumping for joy when he sees you, the manner can be rude or overwhelming, especially for guests. Given the medium-large size of Coonhounds, it's safer for them if your dog knows how to say hello in a less overbearing manner.

The best way to iron out this behavior with Coonhounds is through use of treats. Firstly show him the treat which should be small enough to fit in your palm. Hold it over him, and say "Sit!" once your hand is above his eyes. So long as you get the distance between his head and your hand right, the dog will not jump up.

If he couldn't quite nail the sitting motion, this exercise should render it concrete. When he does sit down, give him the treat and a compliment - "Good dog!"

Importantly you shouldn't start petting your dog. If your dog rises and you start petting he'll feel you're rewarding his rising, not his sitting. Repeat this process a few times until you feel the dog has a comfortable sense of what "sit" means.

Stage two of sitting is to get him to obey the command. You should hold a treat in your right hand for him to smell. Place two fingers of your left hand through his collar, and tell him to sit. If he does so you can give a treat.

Keeping repeating this collar motion until your dog starts to sit without you needing to hold his collar lightly anymore. Every time he successfully sits on hearing the command, you can give him another treat and offer some verbal praise.

Thereafter, reinforcement should be on a strictly random basis. Training should be consistent but also spontaneous: using random intervals in different scenarios not only acts to refresh your Coonhound's mind but also tells you just how comfortable he is in obeying, no matter what the situation.

7) Staying and Going Down

As you progress beyond the first stage of sitting, you'll find yourself rapidly becoming acquainted with your dog's personality. Coonhounds tend to be lively and eager, and this nature can either meld well with training or act to make it more intensive and challenging. Whilst the breed is intelligent, this can equate to a compliant attentiveness or an independent attitude.

Try to time your sessions as you introduce "stay" as your second command as a way in which to keep track of success. You should aim for a steady decrease between new commands, starting at this one. Complete mastery is absolutely necessary before you advance if the training is to go smoothly.

Assume a straight posture and have your dog sit down on your left, but with you facing the same direction - the 'heel' position. Your Coonhound's upper shoulders and head should be parallel to your hip. Attach the training collar and leash. Put the leash's loop over your thumb and fold it into your hand. The leash string should emerge out of the bottom of your hand.

Now you'll need to put your other hand close to the close to the dog's collar. With your hand in place, pull the leash with your other hand to apply tension; note that this shouldn't hurt or discomfort your dog. Use your free hand now; have your palm face the dog in front of the dog's nose - say "stay" whilst making a side-to-side waving motion.

Throughout this time, tension should be maintained on the collar. Make a sidestep to the right, count to ten, and return to your dog. Relax your pull on the collar, offer praise, release your Coonhound, and take several steps forward. Your dog should remain still and attentive through this time.

Now repeat the same steps but from another angle. Rather than stepping to the side, step in front of the dog and again mentally count to ten. Go back to heel, release the tension, offer praise and let go of the dog.

Adjust the collar so that the ring is beneath your dog's chin. Fold part of the leash into the palm of your hand but allow for some slack. Again step back but remain facing your dog with your other hand at your side open palmed.

As you navigate this process, make sure your dog remains attentive. If he's shifting about or looking around distracted, he'll likely get up and go any second. Your Coonhound should be focused solely on you. When the focus drops you should enforce the principle by tugging your leash upwards. Do not speak, instead relax your posture and smile approvingly once your dog's attention is back on you.

If movement does occur, you must take a step towards your Coonhound with your right foot forward. Pull the leash directly above the dog's head without straining the Coonhound's neck. He'll sit back down. Step back into your original place but at no time repeat the word "stay".

Steadily increase the count once you've stepped back. Eventually you should be able to count up to a minute with your dog remaining still and attentive. Try to repeat these steps and introduce five second increments on a steady basis. Once your "stay" count is concluded, about turn and assume the heel position on the right hand side of the dog. Wait a few further seconds (ensuring the sit and stay remains) and then give praise.

This is more difficult and requiring of perseverance than "sit" and it's very likely your dog will get up and walk about until you've managed to deduce his mannerisms. Don't be surprised if your reaction times are too slow at first. Restart the process and make mental notes of the behavior. With patience you should attain mastery of the skill

8) Releasing

Releasing your dog signals that the time for his obedience is over. Your dog is free to move and do as he wishes once you've uttered the word you've given. As with any command, take care not to make a habit out of repetitions - use other means, such as your leash or your posture, to assert yourself. Releasing your dog is simply giving a sign for him to ignore you and go about his day.

A great word to use to signify release is 'okay'. The short simplicity of this word confers a neutrality. You shouldn't round off a training session by exhorting your dog to move with verbal praise. Should you do this, it will act to confuse the dog in the long run and deprive you of a useful verbal cue.

9) Down!

Prior to accomplishing this command you should ensure co-operation is forthcoming. If not you can physically place your Coonhound down in a gentle way. Don't push hard, but instead carefully lift him to the 'begging position' where the hind legs are forced beneath the rear.

Once your dog is there, lower him down to the ground by keeping the forelegs outstretched. If he gets up after this, place him back until he knows to stay. Practice these motions until the dog is comfortable with laying down in front of you. Ideally you should get him to the point of spontaneously laying down for 30 minutes.

Since you've already learned to enforce both sitting and staying in combination, you should also learn how to induce a state of laying down on the same terms. This will prove very useful later when you want to move on to tricks.

Once your dog is sitting on your left in the classic heel position, place two fingers through his collar but keep your palm facing away from his head. Show the dog a treat and lower it down towards the floor. At the same time press gently on the collar to encourage your dog to follow the treat downwards.

When your dog reaches the ground, give the treat to him and offer praise – "good dog!"

At first you should be quite generous with the praise you offer, letting the dog know that this motion now ensures you're happy with him. Practice by at first loosening pressure on the collar, before stopping it entirely. Once your dog can lie down on command and require no verbal affirmation for at least half an hour, you're fine.

With any of these tricks you can bring fun and excitability to the table. Practicing each regularly with the use of treats is important if your Coonhound is to remain consistent. Make your tone and posture lively and keep to the principle of randomness: even outside training sessions can test your dog in different scenarios.

Perhaps the best time to affirm you've a handle on things is when you're exercising the dog. Coonhounds are at their most excited then, surrounded by smells and sights they don't live around. If the above commands are obeyed in the midst of this, you're on the right track.

10) House Training and Crates

One of the most important aspects of life for your dog is house training. Use of crates is vital if this process is to go smoothly, especially with Coonhounds whose boisterousness can grow hard to handle during the later stages of puppyhood.

An unfortunate conception exists amongst dog owners that crates are inhumane; effectively prison cages which confine a puppy and serve to dehumanize the pup's existence in your home. This however is totally untrue.

Dogs carry intact the wolf tendency to make and enjoy sleeping in dens. Such dens in the wild are nothing more than sheltered holes in undergrowth, in outcrops of dirt or rock or beneath fallen trees. Universally they are small - yet wolves live, sire puppies and sleep in them. They provide mental and physical comfort, and mean you can know where your pup is.

So it is with crates, which are effectively a manmade alternative to this existence. Consider also their use in veterinary centers: a puppy or dog unaccustomed to crates can be unhappy in unusual surroundings. Should your Coonhound be hurt somehow, a crate is an ideal and safe place for recuperation. Given that sometimes the house must be empty - a danger with Coonhounds given their spontaneity and love of company - you can use a crate for an hour or two to keep your dog comfortable and non-chaotic. Think of it as a simple 'dog sitter'.

A command is often needed as you introduce your puppy to a crate. "Go to bed" can be useful. If your pup is reluctant to enter, you can place him there whilst speaking the command. Close the door, compliment your pup and hand over a treat.

Afterwards you can use a treat each time you'd like the dog to enter, repeating the process until he understands. Toys can also work to lure the puppy in. After a while he'll enter his crate without any prompting; you're only needed to close the door at night. It's still important to give treats and praise to encourage the behavior. Never use the crate to punish the dog, as it can make the puppy associate it with punishment and discourage him from entering.

Adjusting your anticipation of excretion (in trainer terminology 'elimination') is important as your puppy ages. Every month of your puppy's life equates to about an hour of management of excreta the pup can manage. At six months it's unrealistic to expect intervals of over four hours in the daytime given how busy and active the puppy will be. Digestion is speedy with puppies, meaning a schedule is necessary to manage when he relieves himself.

Routine is vital here; both you and the dog require it. Time precisely when you feed your pup, and stick to it. Four meals a day until the pup is aged four months should be given and can, if you wish, coincide with your own, with the addition of a snack between lunch and dinner or at suppertime.

After those hectic early months you should switch to only two meals a day. This will keep your dog's elimination regular enough to make housetraining manageable but not overwhelming. Ensure that your dog's weight is stable. Coonhounds should be stocky but lean. Loose stools indicates overfeeding, whilst dry ones accompanied by marked straining equates to underfeeding.

Always keep track of your pup's eating. Don't leave him to it, as that can make for distraction. Essentially you should keep this schedule as strict as possible. Provide water in the crate and in the feeding area at all times in the day. At night, remove these dishes so that your dog can sleep without urinating.

Toilet areas must be straightforward and accessible. Away from the house in a straight line (such as out to the back of the garden) is best. Use your leash throughout the process. Coonhounds will likely prove circumspect and will want to sniff about. Be patient and allow for concentration without interrupting.

Once your pup has done his business, compliment him and play for a little while. At the end of your play, hand over a treat. This associates the housetraining with the outside enough for your dog to remember that outside in that location is where he should go.

That you see this happening and follow the relieving with play is important. You must spend time outside, or your dog will assume that going indoors is acceptable. Accompaniment through the whole process is important until the schedule is well-developed. Repetition is key.

If you have a large amount of fenced land as a yard you can allow for your dog to excrete with some freedom as to location. However, you should get into the routine of picking up after him using disposable gloves or a poop scoop. Keep hold of the leash until you're done. In preparation for his doing his business in public on walks you can say "Hurry now" or simply "Hurry" to speed the process. Introduce this gradually after the housetraining is already clear.

The best time to do housetraining is right after your dog wakes up when still in his crate. For puppies, half an hour after eating and drinking is useful too. After playtime, when your dog is worked up, can be good too. A sure sign with Coonhounds is running in circles whilst sniffing the floor. Essentially you need a schedule which minimizes accidents.

If accidents do occur, recall the rule we went over earlier - do not punish after the act. If you have gotten mad before, the 'guilt' will be anticipation of you finding the mess and being mad rather than his regret at making the mess. Move your pup out of sight and clean the area with white vinegar or for certain surfaces a stain remover.

11) Travel and Marking

Travelling should be no impediment to training or housetraining. Even when far from home, proceed as you would ordinarily and make sure your pup is in his crate during the journey. Liveliness is often a given on car journeys. You should be sure you can make a stop every two hours. For adults this isn't as much of a concern. Escort your Coonhound to a discreet area and use your command to make the process quicker.

Once at your destination, the other commands you've mastered can be used too. If visiting someone, make sure you discuss a good area for your dog to do his business. Simply put, you should replicate the home routine as closely as you can.

Marking is another behavior from your dog's wild ancestors. Males and females can engage in this, with vertical places, from bookshelves to fence posts to direction signs popular with the males, who also tend towards these acts with greater frequency. Neutering can, however, vastly reduce the marking done.

Marking's purpose is to mark territory. Instinctual, as it is, it cannot be trained out of a dog. It can be embarrassing in public but should be tolerated. However if you see it happening inside the house or in some other inappropriate place like on your car, you should call the dog's name. After this immediately take him outside and have him relieve himself.

Rare as this is, should marking emerge anew, be sure to restart housetraining. As your Coonhound gains his adult teeth regression can occur. If however the regression persists and you're unable to housetrain again, it could be a medical issue requiring a visit to the vet.

12) Advancing Further

Hopefully the basics we've covered here should propel you to train your Coonhound further. Whilst they do not tend to be so flexible and obedient to perform well at dog shows, they can certainly learn some tricks and more complicated commands.

If you can work on a new one on average once a month, by the time your Coonhound is in his prime, he'll know more than fifty words. Use your imagination and slowly work in hand signals to supplement what you've taught verbally, through use of a collar and through treats. Eventually your dog will associate your signals with motion, and will take to moving to the point where he'll observe just your hand alone regardless of vocalizing.

As with all training, the key is persistence. You can buy handbooks or inquire with other dog owners about tricks and special commands. Coonhounds require perseverance by nature, and this goes double for advanced training and tricks. They do however have intelligence, and the added advantage of being a sight to behold when truly accomplished with training.

13) Adult Training

Coonhounds can be trained in adulthood, although I do not recommend trying to do so from scratch unless you're already experienced with the breed and the tendencies therein. When acquiring an adult, there should already be a familiarity with basic commands and a good adherence to them.

If not, however, you can use the methods above to ensure the dog adapts. Sometimes a mature dog can even adapt quicker owing to honed hearing and an evener temperament. In the case of housetraining, an adult is at a definite advantage - the digestive system is fully developed, meaning that the control of the hound is superior. The urge to eat is better harnessed and the twice a day routine with meals can be observed, rendering the scheduling process easier to establish.

Chapter 6. Home Care, Medical Care And Safety

As well as the essentials of proper medical care, there are many principles you should endeavor towards in order to maximize the quality of life your Coonhound can enjoy. In this chapter we'll cover a wide range of preventative measures which can minimize the need for you to take on the services of a vet with the exception of regular check-ups.

In this chapter we'll cover allergies, proper home care, emergency treatment you can give and what to do during vet visits. Neutering and spaying will also be looked at. A strong daily schedule together with good hygiene can reduce instances of fleas, worms or other parasites as well as making your dog much more pleasant to play and exercise with.

Coonhounds have the advantage of a robust constitution and minimal ingrained issues. However that doesn't mean you can get lax. Like any dog, they can injure themselves accidentally, eat something harmful without thinking, or have allergies you mightn't know about.

We'll cover suggestions for both puppyhood and adulthood in this chapter. Bathing arrangements for instance must change over time given that an adult Coonhound is large. Combining play and fun with essential cleaning duties from the puppy months means you won't end up chasing your dog from the moment he sees the bubbles or smells the soap!

Some dogs go through life free of disease and calamity. Whilst observing the contents of this chapter won't guarantee good health, it will at least increase the likelihood of it.

1) Cleaning Products

Good cleaning, whilst not needed too frequently, remains vital for your Coonhound. As a rule you should engage in bathing when needed or once a week. This can mean after a vigorous time outside after the dog has been in the dirt, or when he starts to smell.

Dog shampoo and conditioner needn't be complex, differing only from human equivalents by their pH balance. You don't need multiple kinds to deal with a Coonhound's short coat. Nowadays there's are all kinds of shampoos and conditioners around which aren't harsh. Try using ones specifically marketed towards shorter coats, and, at least initially, opt for a tearless variety to make yourself comfortable. You can also find ones designed to bring out your dog's color.

A strong, cotton cloth is required, as are two large towels. The dog can stand on one, whilst you use another to dry him. You needn't use your blow-dryer or buy one specially made for dogs so long as you give your Coonhound's coat a good scrub down with the towel.

Cotton balls are vital for the dog's ears. A frequent issue with Coonhounds, and scent hounds generally, is the ears' proneness to infection. You can also opt for a small cloth and coat it in baby oil. Keep them free of dirt and grime, but be sure not to press the cotton balls too far inside in case a piece dislodges.

A good bath brush is useful. If you think it necessary, you can use a pair of dog clippers to trim around the tail. Since this is a minimal job, a cheap pair will serve you well.

2) Choosing a Vet

A vet should essentially be a neighbor whom you can talk to easily about all things dog. By this I mean that the vet centre shouldn't have too clinical an atmosphere. It should be a relaxing place, but clean, tidy and odor free. Remember that Coonhounds get be distracted by strong smells.

Personality wise you'll want someone who is personable, a good listener and readily affectionate with your dog. Politeness should be a given. You shouldn't feel hurried or in a rush to explain problems, and should be comfortable bringing up matters such as costs. A compassionate vet will often offer to group everything, vaccinations, examinations, surgery etc in a single straightforward deal. There should be an air of practical concern and polite probing. They should tolerate your questions, and listen to you talk about your Coonhound with an attitude of receptiveness and learning.

Equally concerning is just how busy it is there - as a rule making an appointment on a weekday is best to avoid a hectic atmosphere since weekends are frequently busy. In any case you should emerge from the surgery confident that neither the reception staff nor vet are overwhelmed with work and trying to fit in as much as possible.

Coonhounds are uncommon in inner-city places, so you'll likely be choosing from vets who are rural or in the outer urban areas. This can carry the advantage of a more varied skill set and well-adjusted temperament: rural vets often tend to farms along with pets. Although an experienced vet is great, remember that you cannot judge on age and should instead observe the walls for certifications or just ask polite questions.

Generally vets will serve those within a five mile radius of their clinics. You can always call ahead and ask to check out the surgery with your dog on a social call of sorts. Short of acute illness or calamity, you'll be looking at visiting the vet's surgery about every six months for a check-up. Morning appointments are best so that the staff aren't fatigued, and it can be wise to make a list - mental or on paper - of questions and points you want to raise.

3) Neutering & Spaying

To neuter a male or spay a female is to prevent reproduction from occurring. Known as 'altering' collectively, for many owners it's a big decision. The effects upon a dog's temperament can't be doubted. Since you're considering a Coonhound as a pet rather than as a part of a pack of working, hunting dogs, it's good to ask yourself whether you'd really want puppies or fear that a male might impregnate a neighborhood dog.

If you live in a one dog home or one where the dogs are all of a single gender, the problem essentially becomes a matter of control. Urges to mate are natural, although a well-trained dog will respond better should you have to call him off approaching or trying to mount another in the vicinity.

However this is easier said than done. Coonhounds are experts at escaping homes. Keeping a untreated dog means redoubling your efforts at closing any conceivable escape route. Even then, the dog can burrow his way under a fence with surprising speed. If they feel the need they will do all they can to take flight and mate. You can't be around them 24 hours a day, and it can be both traumatic for you as an owner and problematic for whoever owns the other dog or dogs too.

If you decide to spay or neuter your dog, be sure to do so early. The effects on the dog's metabolism and weight are negligible so long as you adjust diet and exercise regimen. If you accomplish the dog's neutering during the puppy months, you'll have a far easier time keeping a schedule together.

The earliest possible time for neutering and spaying is about two months, although the process is usually undertaken when the dog is between six and nine months old. Adulthood is no barrier to the process, although the medical benefits can be reduced or non-existent should the dog be over a certain age.

a) Neutering

If you happened to obtain your Coonhound pup at a shelter, it can be that they'll offer to neuter the dog for you. If you bought your Coonhound however you can take your dog to a specialized clinic for about $150 to $250 (£120 to £180) .

Ideally neutering should be done during puppyhood or during early adulthood. If the procedure is accomplished prior to about age four, the likelihood of testicular cancer, prostate-related illness and spikes of unpredictable aggression are much reduced.

b) Spaying

Females especially, will have risks of uterine illnesses and breast cancer reduced if they are spayed prior to when they first enter heat. The spaying process should ideally be done prior to the female reaching adulthood.

As with males, the process can be accomplished in some shelters which offer the service to the pups and young dogs they offer. Failing that there are the aforementioned clinics.

c) Effects On Temperament and Weight

It is a myth that neutering and spaying constitutes an impairment to your dog. The ethical benefits of removing the worry of unwanted pregnancies in your home and in the neighborhood cannot be stated enough. One reason so many dogs end up in shelters or even euthanized is due to their being from an unwanted litter.

Coonhounds are known for their forceful tendencies when outside. The potential for them to strain against a leash to run off in search of the opposite gender is less likely to happen if the dog has been altered. In males the same applies for inappropriate and embarrassing mounting, not just of other dogs, but of people and even random objects. That said, the mating tendencies will not completely diminish in males and the frequent jumping and mounting seen during play will not cease given that it's common for your dog to simply have fun behaving that way.

Aggressiveness may be reduced but it is by no means a given dominance. In theory males in particular would not vie for dominance either physically or as a display with other dogs once the desire for display has diminished. However, Coonhounds can become aggressive out of excitability, or through feeling they should defend you, or through guarding their food from interference by other animals.

Neutering should never be thought of as a cure-all for bad habits and aggression and pursued with that in mind. It should be considered primarily as a method to prevent breeding in the interests of both your personal welfare and that of the animal.

Due to the hormonal changes brought on by neutering and spaying, weight gain may result. However if you've undertaken the process during the dog's early life, the transition to a somewhat less imposing diet, together with a good exercise regime can easily counter such a shift in metabolism. The Coonhound's innate demands when it comes to exercise mean that an extra 15 to 30 minutes together with care over diet can actually be a kindness to the dog, reducing the cause for rowdiness, aggression or the dreaded excess barking.

d) Effects On Roaming and Escape

Coonhounds are perhaps the most notorious breed when it comes to their escaping from your home. When they choose to, they can accomplish impressive leaps, demolish barriers, or try digging under walls for hours at a time, all to leave your home.

Once again, intervening early with your dog is advised to curb this behavior. Having a secure yard prior to the procedure can reduce the appeal of trying in the first place. Most Coonhounds will try escaping even if neutering has occurred. However the frequency and voracity of the process will likely be much reduced. They'll roam around your garden with far less of an expansive enthusiasm, often opting to favor a smaller area as their own.

It's important that your dog hasn't escaped already. Neutering or spaying will almost certainly fail to reduce his boldness.

e) Other Points

Given the existing lack of predisposition to illness in the Coonhound, neutering and spaying can be practiced without fear of arousing a risk that would otherwise have remained dormant.

One frequent event that might even be subconscious is an owner feeding a dog more out of guilt. This can encourage very speedy weight gain, which can lead to a number of issues both medical and to do lifestyle. Keep a close eye on the size of meals and set yourself a limit on daily treat giving during training.

Sometimes dogs can neglect or even apparently forget their housetraining, taking to eliminating in inappropriate spots. If this occurs you should begin the routine of housetraining anew. However, in the long term, the absence of hormonal pressures can mean housetraining reversions become far less common.

4) Vaccinations

Vaccinations are a necessary part of your dog's life and should be pursued in the interests of preserving health. The illnesses vaccines seek to prevent can prove oppressively expensive to deal with and may necessitate putting the dog to sleep.

Something to bear in mind is that the goal of many vaccines is not to rule out illness altogether, but rather decrease the severity with which they occur.

Over vaccination can be a problem, although recently studies have disproved the claim that thyrioditis - inflammation of the thyroid - can occur when a dog has been vaccinated many times over. The controlled study showed the malfunction was not related to repeated vaccinations.

A common concern which you should bear in mind is that not all vaccines last forever. Some require booster shots to complete the respective course, whilst others require a wholesale renewal in order to maintain the effectiveness for the duration of your dog's life.

Fortunately for Coonhounds, the tendency to genetic illness is very slight. This means you can select the needed vaccines without having to become stressed over the risk of certain shots. Several of the commonly employed vaccines have what's termed a 'puppy series', followed by annual boosters. These will be noted in the pages to follow.

Since Coonhounds require so much outside exposure to enjoy a healthy life, vaccinations become necessary. Their interactions with a variety of environments and other animals throughout life renders them needful. If you're concerned and wish to check on your dog's existing immunity you can have a blood test for antibody levels after a year or two.

Vaccinating whilst your dog is still a puppy is important. The early months of a dog's life carry the highest risk and poorest defense against diseases. Since exercise in the country or on parkland is a vital part of a Coonhound's life, it's important to be able to undertake this facet with peace of mind.

Often vaccinations are started when the dog is around two months old, but can be begun as early as six weeks should you wish. The puppy's course is concluded with a second injection two to four weeks along the line.

If your puppy undergoes the majority of core vaccines from this young age, protection can be attained prior to the dog reaching three months of age.

a) Administering A Vaccine Yourself

You can administer the vaccines yourself at home, thereby saving on vet's bills BUT ONLY IF YOU ARE EXPERIENCED AND/OR IF AN EXPERIENCED PERSON SHOWED YOU EXACTLY WHAT TO DO! This procedure is simple, although you should take care to practice.

I do not recommend that you vaccinate your Coonhound yourself. but the reality is that you can now buy vaccinations online and lots of people give their pets vaccines themselves. I am totally against it, therefore I am advising you here of what is important.

Should you decide on administering the dog's vaccine at home, you should familiarize yourself with the procedure. No dog vaccinations are intravenous (into a vein). Instead they are either intramuscular (into a muscle), subcutaneous (beneath the skin) or intranasal (administered through the nose).

Once you have obtained the vaccine vials and a set of sterilized needles, you should insert one needle into the liquid vial. Observe whether or not the vial is multi-dose; if it is multi-dose you should withdraw 1ml.

If you happen to have a second vial containing a powder or freeze-dried vaccine portion, you should inject the liquid into this. Once done, remove the needle and shake the vial of vaccine mixture for a few seconds to ensure the materials properly mix.

After you're done, insert the needle back into the vial and then withdraw the entire mixture to the syringe. If you happen to withdraw an excessive amount of air, you can simply inject this back into the vial. Finally, remove the needle and get ready to inject your dog.

Most vaccines are subcutaneous. A good area to administer the dose is beneath the shoulder; Coonhounds have loose skin over either shoulder. Make sure you don't inject too close to the dog's shoulder blades, and instead lift the skin and commence to insert the needle. Be sure to then pull back on the plunger to check for any blood entering the syringe. If any has, it means you've accidentally pierced a blood vessel, meaning you should withdraw the needle and try a different place.

Intramuscular injections are more difficult without practice. If you are a beginner, it may be wise to consult a veterinarian to administer this form of vaccine. Some vaccines must be delivered to a muscle, else they won't work.

It's important that you only use a needle once per vaccine. After administering a few shots it is often wise to wait a few days so that any soreness or inflammation can clear up. This way, you can still have the entire range of vaccines provided whilst still respecting the dog's comfort.

b) Specific Vaccinations

Listed below are the core vaccinations most vets will recommend your dog get. All of the maladies below cover the commonest general illnesses that all dogs are prone to.

Adenovirus

A dangerous illness which can potentially lead on to hepatitis (liver disease) as well as kennel cough in dogs. Adenovirus can be prevented by vaccinating against type 1 and type 2.

Canine parainfluenza virus (CPiV)

A dangerously contagious respiratory virus, this illness should be dealt with in early life. Following the puppy series, it requires booster shots every three years.

Canine parvovirus

A contagious virus with a high mortality rate, this is an important illness to vaccinate against. Spread via feces, the infection is particularly dangerous to puppies. Upon completion of the puppy series, the vaccine should be renewed every 3 years.

Rabies

Often for public health reasons a rabies vaccination is legally required. Rabies is a virus which affects a dog's brain and spinal cord, rendering the dog dangerous, aggressive and temperamental with a high tendency to bite humans, including their owners, who may then also be at risk of the virus. After the initial vaccine, a second should be givenafter one year, with booster vaccines administered every three years thereafter.

Leishmaniasis

This disease is brought on by parasitic infection. It is possible for the parasites to infect humans, however no such cases have been reported in the USA. Although the disease occurs worldwide it is commonest in India, the Middle East, and tropical zones of the Americas. Often multiple vaccines are required for specific species of worm.

Lyme's Disease

A bacterial infection caused by various species of ticks, this vaccine is particularly advisable for owners who live in or near tick-infested regions. After vaccinating a puppy, treatment should then be on an annual basis.

Ehrlichiosis and Anaplasmosis

Vaccinations for this tick-transmitted bacterial illness remain in the experimental phase. However a preventative approach of tick and general pest control can guard against potential infection.

Distemper

This viral disease should be vaccinated against once every three years after the puppy series. It can affect multiple organs and progress to be life threatening. This is a very commonly given vaccine.

Canine coronavirus

Spread via feces, this intestinal disease is both dangerous and contagious between dogs. Vaccination should be given as a puppy, and renewed yearly.

Leptospirosis

A serious bacterial infection. Although this can pass with only mild incident, it is also possible that serious effects such as internal bleeding and meningitis can emerge in both humans and dogs. After vaccinating your puppy, a yearly renewal is both available and necessary.

In addition to these, there may be several vaccines relevant to your specific region. Other vaccines administered in puppies include

Giardia, Babesia, and the causative ailment Bordetella, also known as kennel cough. Speak with your local veterinarian to see what else is thought of as necessary.

c) Precautions

Coonhounds are known as the namesake of a neurological disease named Coonhound paralysis.

It can be caused by a modified live-rabies vaccine. The nerves direct certain muscles activity, resulting in paralysis. Use of a serum reaction to raccoon saliva can determine if this illness has emerged as a side effect. Nevertheless the recovery process is long, arduous and expensive.

Since a rabies vaccine is law in much of the developed world, it is advisable to place your dog on a detoxification regimen. Often this can involve branded supplements which must be maintained from a week prior to the injection and for months afterward.

A simpler way to ward off rabies vaccine risks is to feed your dog plenty of Omega 3 supplement, which can be gained from fish oil. You can continue this supplementary regimen for a few weeks. Calcium supplements can also be given shortly before the vaccine is due to be administered.

Coonhounds tend to enjoy a robust and healthy profile. As such it's best to consult with the vet about risks of individual vaccines. Once you've ascertained the risk profile, you should familiarize yourself with the symptoms of adverse reaction. These can include fever, appetite loss, swelling of the face, vomiting, respiratory issues, diarrhea, excessive swelling and hair loss at the injection site.

Always observe your dog for these signs in the days following vaccination. Should any of these things occur, be sure to call the vet immediately.

Chapter 7. Health Issues

Coonhounds are famously healthy dogs. Their history in working and hunting in places where medical care beyond simple first aid is either poor or nonexistent, meant that robust health was high on the list of breeder priorities. Undesirable vulnerabilities as well as genetic disorders were rigorously bred out of the dog over the course of centuries.

Nevertheless your Coonhound can suffer from problems from time to time. Whilst many can go for a lifetime with no illness or maladies, it is possible for issues to crop up. Many of these are ailments that can affect all dogs which can be prevented through good care, diet and exercise. As we've said, a health guarantee from a breeder is a must. To ascertain a strong genetic profile, you can ask the breeder for records of x-rays given to the parents.

Importantly, Coonhounds lack the vulnerability to joint issues and hip dysplasia which other dogs of their size commonly struggle with through adulthood. The breed has long since adapted to the pressure brought by vigorous jumping and running. The expense of pressure upon the legs can therefore be maintained under quite late in life, with the Coonhound becoming renowned for a resistance to orthopedic frailty.

However, the absence of vulnerabilities does not mean the dog is immune to most issues, as we'll now cover.

1) Common Problems

Most commonly, Coonhounds struggle with ear infections and certain allergies. Their floppy ears can not only harbor a lot of dirt but can act to insulate and warm their inner ears. Whilst this can act to comfort a dog who is otherwise non-resistant to cold, it can also offer a breeding ground for bacterial and fungal infections.

Ideally you should maintain a weekly schedule in which you check the ears. If you suspect an infection is present it can be prudent to either check with the vet or commence a course of antibiotic medication administered with food. Regardless, you should give the ears a good clean with cotton balls and a cloth dipped in baby oil to ensure hygiene is maintained. The jowls should also be subject to this procedure, as well as the ears themselves being purged of any dirt and grime.

You should also dry the ears thoroughly after bathing, or if the dog happens to get wet otherwise. Keeping the ears dry can rapidly delay onset of yeast or bacterial maladies.

The other common issue with Coonhounds is allergies. Often your dog will take to licking paws, itching and chewing the skin if suffering from these. You should be alert to this behavior; if it persists to the point in which fur is missing and skin reddened, this can mean infection is around the corner.

Allergies can be from a range of things: garden fertilizers and lawn growth promoters, all sorts of foods, even household chemicals found in deodorants or air fresheners. Additionally some flea bites can lead to allergic reactions.

Fortunately you can determine your dog's precise allergies through testing at the vets. Failing that there are cheaper methods such as use of an air filter in the interior of the the room where you see the dog most. Sometimes the problem can simply be a skin infection caused by bacteria, whereupon you should try cleaning with a shampoo designed for that purpose.

2) Congenital Defects and Uncommon Problems

The Coonhound is famously free of genetic defects. However there have been rare instances of hip dysplasia, namely a deformity of the tibia, developing in Redbone Coonhound pups. The deformity usually becomes evident at the age of six months.

Luxating patella, otherwise known as dislocation of the kneecap, has happened in Coonhounds from time to time. No particular breed stands out in this respect, but it can happen from time to time and will become evident when the dog is between four and six months of age.

Studies into congenital disorders occasionally mention various breeds of Coonhound, but the occurrences of rare disorders tend to be anomalies. Rarely, Bluetick and Plott Coonhounds can suffer from rare cellular disorders as well as hemophilia.

Rarely Coonhound paralysis may strike. Although it shares the Coonhound name, this disease is no commoner in Coonhounds than it is in many other breeds of dog. If you do take your Coonhound for walks in wooded areas or areas known for their raccoon population, it would be wise to keep them on a leash - not only can raccoons contribute to the paralysis mentioned, they can also physically wound or bite your dog in a scuffle.

3) Pet Insurance

Pet insurance for purebred Coonhounds is often higher due to the absence of 'hybrid vigor'. Despite the strong health profile, many insurers will not categorize their premium costs based on individual breeds.

Nevertheless in case of calamities it is wise to insure your pet. Treatment costs can run into the thousands of dollars, and given the variety of energetic activities you'll undertake with your Coonhound, it's wise to pick up some insurance relatively early in life.

Chapter 8. Temperament

Coonhounds are famous for their even-tempered but active ways. Given their independence they'll often strike out a unique personality. Sometimes their affection towards children and people is so strong they'll forget their size and tumble about. As a pet the Coonhound shines as a member of a family. They can share in joy and pain, and are intuitive about emotions in a watchful, intelligent manner. They enjoy, react to and require nature around them, their happiness determined by a good home and green surroundings.

So much of the dog's life revolves around exercise. The Coonhound is up there with the most energetic breeds in terms of how much they'll end up walking the Earth. If you've a few extra pounds you'd like to shed, rest assured the Coonhound will see you to fitness. His persistent bawls and barks do a better job than any aerobics or fitness instructor could. This is part of the dog's nature which you cannot and should not stop; a healthy Coonhound is built upon physical effort.

Barking or bawling in a voice that might even border on the tuneful is another habit which Coonhounds cannot be prevented from doing. They'll joyfully bark for hours, and very loudly.

A creative but patient heart is needed to properly cater and find a Coonhound rewarding. The essentials of the dog do not vary, although there is definitely variance in individuals. Treated properly a Coonhound can come to respect a time when exercise has to be lighter, or when a family member is under the weather, or when he has a friend of yours sitting him whilst you take a break.

1) Behavior Towards Children and Pets

Coonhounds are underrated when it comes to their abilities as family pets. Many supposed experts regard them as simply hunting dogs, fit only for a life spent roaming about or sitting around a kennel outside a hunter's cabin. Nothing could be further from the truth however. Coonhounds are wonderful with children and, if properly trained, other pets.

A bugbear which often crops up with the dog is his behavior towards small animals, particularly cats. Bred to hunt and see smaller creatures as something to be chased and caught, means this tendency is in his blood. Adapting his attitude to any pets you have in the home can be done however.

Perhaps the most straightforward way to have him accept other animals in the home is to familiarize him with them right away. A big benefit of having a puppy over an adult is the Coonhound's manner in accepting them. He'll be tolerant and respectful to creatures he grows up with.

If you desire to introduce a new pet of diminutive size, be sure to discipline your Coonhound should he ever attempt aggression. The first months of owning another pet require vigilance on the part of those in the home. In order for his obedience and respect for you as his owner to surpass his instincts, you must exact scorn immediately if any aggression or fights start.

Despite this drawback it's important to recall that Coonhounds value a sense of belonging and family above most things in life.

They'll respect people and children and have a near-limitless energy when engaging in play and exertion. Eventually your dog will become part of the furniture, and your schedule and treatment of him so routine that it's second nature.

2) Do Coonhounds Carry A Tendency To Escape?

Yes! Not only do they escape, they do so with a creative tenacity which can surprise owners. If you let them escape once, you can be sure they'll do so again and again. When they run back to the house they'll often be happy, tail wagging and looking at you with a senseless joy. They've just had a fine afternoon and are thinking: "What an amazing day! Won't master be happy I'm happy?"

To Coonhounds, escape is an achievement. It's something they put a lot of work towards. Digging for hours, strategically jumping on top of walls or objects in sequence, or even destroying pieces of barrier or fence can all be part of a great game. They'll team up with other dogs, and even when well-trained will not be deterred from this hobby.

On the one hand it can be worrying when escapes happen. It can mean expense, hand-wringing about the dog's whereabouts, or a well of anger building which you can't unload on the dog as he'll not understand. In serious cases it is possible the Coonhound will simply keep following smells for many miles, often ending up discovered far away from home days later.

On the other hand, it's a sign that something needs to be done. This doesn't necessarily mean extra fence posts, a border of paving flags or poured concrete, or other physical deterrents. It doesn't mean blindfolding your dog on walks so that the outside seems less appealing either. It can simply mean that there's something missing in the dog's life. Often escapism can be curbed simply by playing for 15 minutes, or lengthening walks, or even just training the dog to relax with you for a time.

Effectively you want your Coonhound to think about other things. Occupying the dog is a responsibility best shared between family members. Jigging around the schedule is doubtless something you'll want to do should attempts persist. Interrupting him in the act can, as with all bad behaviors, be good - but primarily you should be concerned with incentive and alternatives over scolding.

Chapter 9. Grooming

Despite the short coat which characterizes all breeds of Coonhound, the need for good general grooming is just as much a reality as with any other dog. Though care needn't be frequent, a Coonhound's requirements are not simply to keep up appearances. Proper tending to the ears, eyes and coats, for instance, can act to prevent infections and minimize the risk of such ailments as ticks and fleas. The likelihood of parasites finding their way inside your dog is likewise dramatically reduced.

Keeping your dog's teeth in a good state not only determines how well your pet can eat, but also minimizes the risks of infection. Just as a person's mood can be upset through toothache, so too can a dog's. Likewise a good bath can, for a person, be a quick route to feeling better and more relaxed as well as more clean. It's the same for a Coonhound - a well-disciplined, behaved dog won't kick up a fuss during bath time.

A presentable Coonhound of any breed can act to impress. Despite not being valued as show dogs, a well-kept Coonhound can be striking given the animal's bearing and innate tendency to fitness. Once you factor in a clean appearance and odor, the dog's innate charm can really come out and prove a good talking point with those around you. A clean, fresh smelling dog is received well by other dogs too, and is much more pleasant a companion to be walking with for a couple of miles each day.

1) Grooming Ground Rules

As with training, exercise and even feeding, grooming requires compliance. Effectively you must make a deal with your dog. The best way to ensure this is to start early, when the Coonhound is still a pup. Given that this is a Coonhound, expect some reluctance when you begin and to be giving treats as you would when training.

You must use the training, especially sit, down and stay in the grooming process. As with use during exercise, grooming can be a real test of whether the commands have stuck. The dog must be stationary throughout, and must not make attempts to get away or, as with bathing, try to shake off the suds.

Make sure you've bought the full complement of equipment. Brushes, nail clippers, dog toothbrushes, bath tubs and so on. Speaking of bath tubs, remember that grooming should only take place in your kitchen sink if your dog is a puppy. It sounds obvious but people can and have tried bathing large dogs that way.

Keep a diary so you don't miss a session. Combining both washing with grooming on a single day is not only convenient but can, over time, act to teach your dog about what will happen sequentially.

2) Bath Time!

The cornerstone of cleanliness for any dog is a good bath. Despite the short fur, Coonhounds should be bathed as needed. Usually this means after they've spent time in the dirt or once they start to smell. Unless either of those things happen more frequently, once a week is fine. Just make sure that your regular bath coincides with the rest of the cleaning you'll be doing.

As well as observing the general rules mentioned above, try not to be in any hurry when doing this and any other task. You should be relaxed, taking your time to tend to your duties whilst making it as fun an experience as possible. Keep cotton balls in your dog's ears to prevent moisture going inside, and use a stool next to your dog's tub in order to keep your back from hurting.

Once every few baths you should express your dogs anal sacs. Otherwise it can be quite unpleasant given that the bad smell and, doubtless, mess can't be washed away. You'll realize the necessity when your dog tries to chew at his butt or even drags it along.

If you forget to do it during bathing, be sure to use paper towels positioned beneath the anus to catch the liquid which may be ejected during the expression. You shouldn't do this too frequently as it can damage the glands surrounding the anus, leading to infection.

Once the tail is pointing upwards, place your fingers in the 4 and 8 o'clock positions around the dog's anus. The liquid should be then be ejected. Be sure to ask your vet about this during an early check-up as you might end up doing this job a bit too harshly.

3) Hair and Toenail Clipping

Hair clipping needs are minimal with your Coonhound. Generally speaking you'll need only to apply clippers to the tail and parts of the feet. Occasionally an odd growth of hair can occur which you can trim back. Your dog's needs are usually minimal in this regard.

Toenails are much more a concern and do need to be tended to from time to time. An exception occurs if you happen to live in a house with plenty of stone floors, and walk your dog upon stone much of the time. This activity acts to wear down the dog's toenails naturally, meaning only the occasional trim is needed. This can be the norm for Coonhounds, who by nature spend a lot of time walking anyhow.

Unfortunately there's no way to render toenail care completely comfortable. This is one part of the grooming process where even a trained dog can kick up a fuss. Trim one paw at a time, or even use a nail file if your dog happens to tolerate that better. If you're confused over the precise length of the toenails optimal for your Coonhound, have a word with a professional groomer or the vet at the next check-up.

Not only does nail clipping increase comfort for your dog in the long run, it can stop your dog accidentally scratching and hurting you or those around you during play. However do not trim too far - the 'quick' fills the base of the dog's nail and will bleed heavily if cut. Cauterization or styptic powder is then necessary to stop the flow. The pain such over-trimming causes the dog can taint future grooming with bad memories.

As always, provided your dog isn't being too naughty during the process, be sure to provide a treat after you're through clipping.

4) Ear Care

Good ear care is the part of grooming most pivotal for the continued good health of your Coonhound. The ears of a Coonhound can easily get clogged with dirt and grime which can then mature into a full-blown bacterial malady requiring medicines and a vet visit. If you notice an odd, slightly pungent odor around the ears, this can be a sign of infection.

After the dog has been thoroughly toweled dry after a bath you can turn to the ears. If you used cotton balls to prevent wetness, after disposing of them you can use two more to scrub out any residual dirtiness. Better still use a small cloth coated in baby oil.

A great way to make ear cleaning go smoothly is to transfer the massaging principles you had during the wash to the ears. With a Coonhound this means gentle handling and even a little light scratching on the parts of the flaps he likes to be scratched.

If you choose to do your grooming after a typically long spell of exercise with the dog, expect an all-round compliant attitude. Sapped of energy, your Coonhound will put up much less of a struggle through the grooming process.

Finally, through the entire process never be rough; gently scour the ears for dirt but do not insert anything hard. As you stroke the flaps of the ears be sure not to pull them or be otherwise rough. Don't bother pulling out any hair that grows internally no matter how unsightly it might look. It hurts the dog and few people will be looking up there anyway.

As with the other steps, at the end hand him a treat and a note of praise.

5) Eye Care

Another universal rule with dogs is that mostly the eyes will look after themselves. Much as human eyes suffer from 'morning glories' - bits at the corners - every other day after sleeping, so too do your dog's.

However it is important that you tend to the cleaning needs from time to time. Coonhounds have quite prominent eyes, making them quite easy to tend to. Bear in mind that if the eyes are reddened or are teary for long periods, this can be a sign of a number of maladies such as ear and dental infections and even tonsillitis.

Whilst people will often spontaneously and easily remove any built up gunk, your dog's paws do not afford him the luxury. As such, quite a bit might have built up over the week since you last tended. A clean cloth or cotton ball can easily get a hold of any such deposits.

It's not nice to have your eye poked, and that goes for your Coonhound too. Other manners which can ensure comfort include a little face massage: rub the jowls and forehead with gentle consideration. Use a soothing tone as you get every bit of dirt and gunk off. This will ensure the dog is comforted and happy as you finish up.

Bear in mind that you can cover this during a bath alongside the entire face. However, the presence of shampoo can act to irritate: even if you think you can exclude it. Remember that only a trace is needed to make your dog's eyes sting. Therefore it's best to clean the face and eyes after the bath itself is done.

6) Dental Concerns

The benefits of keeping your dogs teeth brushed and clean cannot be stated enough. Although dogs don't suffer from cavities in the same manner as humans, they still carry a vulnerability to plaque, tartar and gingivitis which leads to foul breath and general dental problems.

Prevention is as always better than cure. A visit to a pet dentist can be costly, since among the costs present are anesthesia - simply put your dog will not open his mouth and say 'ahhh'. In the case of infections of the jaw and face stemming from poor or non-existent dental care, you can even find your Coonhound ends up suffering organ damage due to the infection spreading through the bloodstream.

As such I recommend a robust and frequent brushing regiment. Many dogs even in modern times go without brushing - although daily would be useful. Realistically, so as to not impact your lifestyle, once a week soon after the other grooming procedures can be fine.

Just as it's best to bathe your dog after he's exercised, so too can this post-exercise lethargy serve to be useful in gaining his co-operation when tending to the teeth.

When commencing to brush the dog's teeth you must train compliance, opening the mouth by folding up your dog's lips either side with one hand. Use your thumb on one side with your hand holding the muzzle, whilst the fingers on the other side of the mouth are wrapped around to the bottom lip.

Initially the dog will recoil or protest. You can watch what he does when you initially touch his mouth, and repeat doing so until he accepts such a light touch. Coonhounds will react well if you feed them a treat just before you do this; as the treat is chewed you can accomplish the motion I just mentioned and touch the gums.

7) General Tips On Dental Care

As with many things concerning dogs, repetition is needed for success. Use of treats and morsels to distract the Coonhound as you practice opening his mouth can be useful as you acclimatize him to having his gums touched. Initially you should simply pull up the folds of skin for a brief time.

Later on you should extend the time. Rub upon the gum tissue with your fingers gently, and to test his restraint use a treat in the other hand. It's also possible to employ flavored canine toothpaste. Slowly you should work in short massages of the gums, at first just a couple of seconds and then lengthened.

The process is slow as a rule and may take a few weeks to master. Once your dog accepts and grows to like such handling, you should use a wet cloth and commence rubbing the teeth. Throughout this process you should gently soothe and use a cooing tone with the Coonhound.

If the dog reverts to impatience as you introduce the cloth, cease the rubbing and give him a treat. As with your finger massage you must then start to lengthen the time you use with the cloth until acceptance is gained.

a) Equipment

You'll need both a special toothpaste and toothbrush for the brushing. Whatever the frequency, from twice a day to twice a month, you should try to make the process enjoyable. Dog toothpastes are given meat flavors which means your pet will have a much better time.

Dog toothbrushes are simple to find in pet stores, and are often termed finger brushes. Whilst use of a human toothbrush is possible, finger brushes are better tailored towards a dog's mouth.

b) Periodontal Disease

One of the biggest fears brushing protects against is inflammatory gum disease. This is one of the commonest ailments a dog suffers from. Progressively spaces can appear beneath the teeth which are then occupied by bacteria which cause decay and damage. Long term there can even be infections of the mouth and jaw resulting from the buildup of bacteria.

c) Teeth Scaling

Increasingly the scaling of the teeth is thought of as a matter that can be done in the home. Effectively you are using a sharp tool to scrape away tartar and plaque buildup. Unfortunately, due to the presence of a sharp instrument, a single jerk from the Coonhound can result in a cut to the gum tissue and pain.

If you believe scaling is necessary it is best to consult a veterinarian with dental expertise to anaesthetize the dog. This also means areas which you'd miss were the dog conscious, can be reached and properly scaled whilst the danger to your pet is minimal.

d) Retained PrimaryTteeth

As is the case in humans, dogs have two sets of teeth. Between about three and seven months in age a dog's permanent teeth will emerge. However some of the 'milk teeth' (aka 'deciduous teeth') can remain behind.

This can be a concern due to an impacted biting pattern which can render eating difficult. In the worst cases the jaw can assume an abnormal position. If you witness an unusual tooth formation in your dog's mouth be sure to tell your veterinarian as it may be necessary for the tooth or teeth to be removed professionally.

8) Skin

A Coonhound's skin should be checked during your grooming session. Often this can mean pushing aside hair on patches that you've observed being scratched or which seem worn. Ailments such as ticks and mites or even fungal infections can happen from time to time. If you discover any such creatures in your Coonhound's coat, do not attempt manual removal but instead use a specialized shampoo specific to dealing with such conditions. Repeat washes may be necessary but eventually the problem will subside.

Alternatively skin issues can simply be the expression of an allergic reaction. Sometimes, if the dog is allergic to pollen, the skin troubles can only happen in summer. A good HEPA filter can at least mitigate this, although you must still expect exposure during one of the Coonhound's lengthy walks.

If you come up short in discovering any insects squatting beneath your Coonhound's fur, it can also be wise to alter your dog's diet. Since allergies can crop up periodically, it's possible it could be a longstanding food you'd assume there's no issue with.

Should the skin remain irritated, reddened or otherwise abnormal you can always go for allergy testing. Visits to the vet for dermatological treatment are expensive, but should be considered if fur loss or skin issues persist despite your efforts.

9) Required Equipment and Supplies

You needn't have a room in which to groom your dog, although it's usually wise to set aside an area. Coonhounds aren't too complicated when it comes to cleaning - they don't need their hair trimming, don't need multiple types of brushes or combs or any fancy conditioners to look good.

As such, it's wise to simply buy what you need. Coonhounds are not by nature a show dog as such. Despite their handsome frame and posture they really don't need a lot of pampering to look their best, and often it's best to simply forget lengthy grooming in favor of more exercise which will often result in a happier dog.

a) Shampoo & Conditioners

Keeping a few different shampoos and conditioners can be useful. Use one of each for general use, but also keep some with you to deal with ticks or fleas. There are also varieties that can be used for sensitive skin, such as when your dog is recovering from a bacterial infection and is still growing back patches of fur.

Given the Coonhound's short coat, you'll be able to economize on using these products. Just use as much as you need, taking care to conserve as much as you can whilst keeping the dog well-cleansed.

b) Styptic Powders

In technical terms styptic powder is an antihemorrhagic product. This means it stops bleeding. You might have seen some in the supermarket advertised for shaving and paper cuts. Often these is available as a pencil of the material which you should apply to the site of the bleeding. It's worth having some of this spare in loose powder form for use in case your dog gets a cut or you accidentally cut off too much of his toenail.

A half ounce of loose powder costs $10-12, whilst a pencil (1/3rd ounce) costs about $3 to $4.

c) Ear Powdering & Cleaning

You can use some powders to dry out and give some grip to the Coonhound's ears. However, usually a simple cloth coated in baby

89

oil is more than enough. If the ears are especially dirty you can use a little water on a cloth gently.

An exception would be if your dog suffers from wax buildup. A heavy presence of wax can make cleaning with cloths prohibitively difficult. If this is the case a good ear powder can make all the difference. Both online outlets and brick and mortar pet stores offer it fairly cheaply.

A 20gram vial costs about $10-12.

d) Canine Toothpastes

As noted, dogs cannot use human toothpaste. Human toothpastes often minty flavors can be repulsive to a dog, as can the foam which develops from brushing with it. A typical dog toothpaste will have a chicken or beef flavoring, and will not have a foaming quality.

A large tube will cost about $6 - $8.

e) Paw Creams

Coonhound paws tend to be tough and bred for plenty of use. Nevertheless if you find them cracked, scabby or bleeding on any occasion it's sensible to buy some paw cream.

A tube costs about $15.

10) Professional Grooming

Although Coonhounds aren't known for their grooming needs, it can be worthwhile to visit a professional groomer a couple of times a year. If you meet a competent individual they will happily offer advice as to aiding your dog's grooming process. If you're already satisfied with how you can manage it personally, don't bother.

A need for such services for Coonhound owners is usually uncommon. It can be worthwhile to visit to simply get the lowdown on the latest products. Mostly, however, you should stick to tending your Coonhound yourself, given that the cost involved in paying for grooming can be rather high.

If you feel you're getting good at grooming and feel you can undertake the service as a way of making money, starting a business from your efforts, bear mind in the Coonhound isn't the best choice for training. Their limited needs mean you simply cannot build your skills. Hairier dogs and the varieties of toy dog are far better kinds of dogs to kick start a fledgling career in grooming.

Chapter 10. Nutrition

To paraphrase a popular phrase, your dog is what it eats. A good, balanced diet makes for a good, balanced Coonhound.

Even by dog standards, Coonhounds are known to simply gobble down their food with a minimum of chewing. Exceptions exist however, with the Treeing Walker hound known to be much more inclined to leanness than his cousins. Before we get to the nitty gritty of nutrition, simply bear in mind that you can properly pace your Coonhound's eating by placing a bunch of stones big enough to not be chewed or swallowed into the dog's food bowl. This obstructs the Coonhound from eating too quickly and minimizes any risk of choking. Likewise if you study food packaging you can gather just how much nutritional value is actually present: flashy, well-designed graphics and pictures of healthy, attractive dogs don't necessarily mean the best nutrition.

When feeding, consider how heavily you exercise the dog. If you devote hours a day to vigorous play and walks as opposed to just quick sessions, adjust your Coonhound's consumption accordingly.

Hydration is vital a Coonhound of any age. Given their exertive ways, they'll lose water quickly even in colder climates and seasons. Just like humans, dogs of any breed will die within days without water to consume. Dogs will take to panting to let you know they're thirsty. You can adjust water consumption according to whether you opt for a wet or dry diet. In some regions tap water is rigorously processed and can be acceptable to drink. If you're suspicious however, you can buy purified water in bulk or conduct a test on your water supply to see if the level of chemicals present is acceptable for drinking.

1) Feeding Puppies

Keeping your puppy fed is important for mood as well as to health. A strong diet will prevent lapses to both illness and bad behavior. Care over a balanced diet is therefore essential. Balancing simple treats with quality meals is a step to ensure your Coonhound pup will grow and thrive.

Be aware that most of the bigger name brands use some of the lowest quality, poorly-sourced meat on the market. As in the kind you wouldn't find even in the cheapest of value burgers. Whilst clean most of the time, the meat's inadequacy is reflected in the nutritional profile and your dog's likelihood of getting bored of it quickly. Variation is vital to keep your Coonhound enthusiastic.

Coonhounds were bred for an excellent sense of smell. This is a dog that can vividly smell the scents of living animals through thick tree thickets and undergrowth for hundreds of yards. Even as a puppy, the odor of food when the food is right under their nose is unimaginably strong to us humans. As such it's best to both vary the diet and opt for premium foods. Expensive brands offer good quality at a price, whilst certain specialty stores will stock foods which mix meat rich in protein, unsaturated fats, and grains stocked with carbohydrates. Often this pricy chow is free of chemical additives, be they hormones leftover from the meat production line or steroids which can lead to temperament issues.

2) Feeding Adults

That your Coonhound has become a healthy young adult does not mean you should switch to cheaper foods. If anything, young adulthood signals a time for experimentation. Freed of the burden of catering to rapid body growth month to month, you can commence to try different diets and foods. An exception you can carry on is simply giving the Coonhound some of the food you eat: avoid anything processed and keep it to fruits, veggies and meat.

Just like humans, dogs have favorite foods. Most will opt for savory treats that are high in protein. Don't take that as a signal you can't try varying things. Although Coonhounds are famously tolerant to change, it's still wise to phase out what you tried previously so as to avoid any discomfort or gastric issues through the transition.

Fine tuning should also be possible once your Coonhound has grown up. Whilst puppyhood should see a gradual increase in what's given, you can experiment to reach a healthy, even plateau for the adult. Since exercise is a daily reality, it's great to keep the dog's energy up by bringing a few treats along.

Regarding meals, if you've opted for tins, remember that you can safely refrigerate a partly full tin for up to 24 hours so long as it's covered. If you tend to eat rice, potatoes or vegetables, try cooking a bit of a surplus and mixing these carb-heavy foods with the tinned food for a good all-round meal. Fresh meat and homemade gravy can be an even better substitute.

If you aren't too mindful of your Coonhound keeping its peak fitness, this kind of regimen can be fine. Coonhounds do not carry much risk of obesity.

3) Things To Avoid

As your Coonhound grows, you might notice they've allergic reactions after some meals. This can range from itching to gastric problems, to persistent skin conditions. If you pay attention to what's fed and attempt a process of elimination for things that are new, you'll soon have a good allergy profile for your dog.

If the problem persists however, you can head to the vet, who may prescribe what's termed a 'hypoallergenic diet' which contains a well-rounded nutritional profile that won't cause harm. You can then, bit by bit, reintroduce foods until the problem is stumbled upon and corrected.

General vulnerabilities to certain foods must be kept in mind. Dairy foods posses enzymes that cannot be digested properly by young dogs: they shouldn't be given to puppies and shouldn't be given in quantity to adults. Otherwise the dog will suffer indigestion and heavy flatulence that can persist for a day or longer.

Overfeeding a Coonhound can be tantamount to cruelty. As with humans, excess food can have an uncomfortable bloating effect which makes activity uncomfortable. Whilst your Coonhound should enjoy and be satisfied with what's offered, overfeeding can act against the breed's nature as an active and generally trim hound.

Poor habits at meal time can develop if you don't keep an eye on things. Make sure that you and those living with you don't habitually throw pieces of meat or scraps from the dinner table. On being ignored in future, the dog may interpret that it must whine or bark for this apparent 'reward' which can be super annoying as you try to eat. Equally important is discouraging competition, aggression or defensiveness with food, which can cause fights between other dogs.

4) Treats To Consider With Caution

Precautions should not stop at only the dog's main diet. Snacks and treats should also be considered. As in meals, moderation is key here. Some snacks can be fine if given sparingly, whilst others are bad no matter what the quantity they're given in.

a) Rawhide

Made from cowhide, the various types of rawhide snack and bones available are inexpensive and widely available. Some dogs find them delicious, chewing upon the coarse material absorbing their interest and strengthening their teeth. It proves a useful distraction from less desirable hobbies and having some as a treat will stick in your dog's mind as a reward for exercise, good behavior and so on.

Bear in mind, however, the unregulated nature of these treats which mean certain varieties can contain harmful bacteria due to poor manufacture and preserving. Coonhounds tend to swallow food with more haste than most dogs which can make rawhide a choking hazard should the Coonhound bite off too much.

It is best to simply observe whether your dog has any difficulty with this type of treat. If so, cease using rawhide as a treat. The same goes if your Coonhound ends up disinterested in his next meal or shows signs of tummy discomfort. Given the choking hazard it is best to dispose of the rawhide when it becomes small.

b) Pig's Ears

These treats carry much the same disadvantages as rawhide. Given their thinner structure they may pose a still greater danger to your Coonhound due to the relative ease of swallowing. As with rawhide, owners have reported the same bacterially provoked problems, given that once again there is no regulation on these treats.

Whilst you may be able to locate a good brand and have a Coonhound who knows how to consume chewy foods without choking, it may be best to cease or strongly curtail buying pig's ears if problems occur.

A further drawback is the sheer fattiness most pig's ears possess. Despite the chewiness, they will mostly digest in a dog's stomach, bringing a lot of fatty calories. This probably won't make much of a difference so long as you indulge your Coonhound in workouts and physical play along with an otherwise rounded diet. If you intend to use pig's ears frequently you ought to consider their fatty profile.

c) Hooves

As with the previous two treats, cow's hooves can be a great snack for certain Coonhounds. Despite their chewiness there are some notable disadvantages.

Firstly the smell tends to be unpleasant and manure-like. If you can tolerate bad odors better than most, this won't bother you. However it is important to keep this in mind for the consideration of others. Another issue is that many hooves can be brittle from the get go, resulting in the familiar choking hazards.

The greatest danger with hooves is the propensity they have to fracture into shards of bone fragments, which many dogs will swallow in their enthusiasm. These shards can cause discomfort to the dog's esophagus and digestive tract and they will show up in the feces. Not to mention the danger of rigorously chewing such tough material - your dog could well crack or lose a tooth. Given the natural enthusiasm of Coonhounds, this is a particular danger.

Any of the three snacks here can be okay on occasion. Many dogs love them. Do bear in mind the pitfalls and think twice when you visit the pet store.

5) Healthy Treats

Fortunately you needn't resort to treats that aren't healthy in order for your Coonhound to enjoy the dental and relaxing benefits of chewing. Healthier treats will also better tackle the common issue of bad breath many dogs suffer.

a) Bully Sticks

One of the most enduringly popular treats on the market, bully sticks consist of bull genitalia melded together to form a dense, ultra-chewy treat. Most dogs will fast gain a liking for these, and can easily while away an evening happily chewing one.

Despite the edibility, bully sticks last through quite heavy chewing. The biggest downside is that they tend to be more expensive than most treats and can easily rival hooves in terms of rank odor, especially after chewing has commenced. However there are low odor varieties that many owners swear by.

b) Flavored Chews

If you want to enhance your dog's dental health it can be sensible to choose a few flavored chews. The benefit of these is that they cut down on odor thanks to being made from processed grains or poultry meal. Given how quickly these can be consumed, especially among aggressive eaters like the Coonhound, you might want to think twice before you opt to buy a bunch.

Another precaution surrounds diet. If you're wishing to keep your dog off grains as part of your nutritional program, it could be best for you to make a different choice unless you've just rounded off an afternoon of strenuous exercise.

c) Healthy Biscuits and Sweet Treats

Biscuits - sweet or savory - can be plenty suitable for your Coonhound. They needn't be loaded with fatty butter or anything elaborate or unsuitable like chocolate chips. Oatmeal biscuits with just a little sugar can be just as delicious for a dog, as well as providing a quick handy source of energy and carbohydrate.

Savory biscuits differ only through exchanging an oat texture for wheat and some form of beef or chicken stock in lieu of butter.

Other sweeter treats include pieces of frozen yogurt combined with peanut butter. There are some treats available which are simply baked fruit bound together with a little oil and molasses.

None of these suggestions pose any health risk unless used to excess. Sugars and fats are fine in moderation, and the memorable taste they give can well aid and motivate your dog to play well, walk and run enthusiastically and just be an all-round good hound.

d) Homemade Snacks

Making snacks, or even mini-meals for your dog, is certainly possible. Simple biscuits can be crafted from 2 1/2 cups of wheat flour, an egg, some water, a stock cube and a pinch of salt. Once the dough is shaped, 30 minutes in the oven at 350 celsius will do it.

Just as people enjoy soups and stews, so do dogs. A small stew can be a brilliant little snack meal with which to treat your dog. Boiling leftover diced vegetables, potatoes, bits of meat in a pan for 20-30 minutes can be a great way to treat your dog on arriving home. If you're alone, timing for your stew can be perfected through use of a slow cooker.

The very same ingredients can be dried rather than boiled to create a dehydrated mixture which is great to bring on outings. This can be accomplished easily by placing the whole shebang in a special dehydrator. For added variety you can also add fruits, raisins excepted.

6) Considerations Towards Food

Your dog will always consider food to be a small gift or token of affection. As an animal a dog has few wants beyond what we'd consider our own basic needs. Food is therefore a big thing to them which is why it is so great to use during training. The size of a treat needn't be a concern; even a small biscuit or morsel tells the dog you approve.

Make doubly sure your dog has been well-behaved and be sure to link the provision of foods with a "Good boy!" or similar compliment. If the dog is behaving too excitedly, is barking, or is otherwise behaving naughtily, then do not grant a treat. Your dog should accept discipline before you pour on affection and praise and should understand that those two principles are very connected.

Ideally, treats and meals should be a way in which to relax your dog. The natural posture is sitting and looking up expectantly at you, perhaps with a wag of the tail should they know it's treat time. If you're exercising your Coonhound rigorously using a long leash, training this response in a good setting such as a park can have you and your dog mutually sensitive.

Coonhounds are especially happy with treats. As hunters born and bred, the taste and quality of food, and especially meats, imbue a sense of attainment. You can exploit this to a very beneficial extent: food and treats properly given is the difference between a decent Coonhound and an exceptional one. If you can be sensibly generous with quality food over the first year of the hound's life, your companion will be all the more devoted.

With all food, even treats, it's wise to read up on what goes into them. A good idea would be to ask your vet to recommend you a given brand or type of food. Age-specific dog foods can be useful at various stages of life, and vets will be very clued in to the best local brands. Nevertheless every dog is different, and you might discover certain favorites years into the Coonhound's life.

a) Dental Matters

Coonhounds boast a robust set of teeth, bred for strength and power through biting motions. Despite the strength of the mandible and teeth in the mature Coonhound, it's important that you take care when tending to the dog's diet. Chewing is great for health and actually assists in removing plaque and tartar in between the times you brush the dog's teeth.

Observing your dog's dental health is another way to fine tune diet. If you notice small cracks or wear it's time to change the food before your dog is in pain. Fractures to teeth may also necessitate a visit to the vet and the expense that entails.

b) A Coonhound's Teeth and Jaw

In some breeds of Coonhound, notably the Treeing Walker and Black and Tan, the teeth should be cleaned more frequently than other breeds due to their general mouth, muzzle and jowl structure.

Coonhounds can manage bones and chewy treats in moderation although consistent monitoring can be favorable. Once the adult teeth have arrived, you should feel more comfortable with providing tougher foods. Some dogs have naturally stronger teeth, though all can benefit from calcium and vitamin supplements aimed at strengthening both teeth and bones.

c) Canine Digestion

Dogs feature a much simpler digestive system than humans. Whereas we savor our food with chewing, weighing up the different tastes and qualities, dogs will simply wolf down their food with a speed that's astonishing by comparison. As such, no digestion occurs until the food gets to the hound's belly. Digestion tends to take between seven and ten hours for adult dogs, and as little as an hour for a puppy.

Coonhounds have a flexible jaw much like most dogs. Its size, together with numbers of teeth and a wide gullet, allow the dog to swallow large morsels of meat and general food. Once the food has reached the stomach it is broken down by huge amounts of hydrochloric acid.

Despite the carnivorous qualities the dog has evolved over eons, a decent quantity of vegetables and fruits can be eaten, especially when mixed with other nutrients including the all-important meat. Once the food has been broken down by the sheer quantity of acid present, it moves onto the dog's small intestine.

Here the nutrients are progressively siphoned, filtered and assimilated. The dog's intestinal tract is lengthy, making both the small and large intestine efficient in their work. The liver contributes bile whilst the pancreas contributes fluid that both aids the process and confers feces its distinct color. Finally once through the system all that remains is for the waste to be built up.

By the time the food has navigated the intestines, it is broken down to the extent where water, undigested matter and some dead bacteria remain. This mass, the feces, passes through the rectum and is excreted through the anal sphincter.

7) Different Diets

There are numerous diets you can introduce to your Coonhound. The two most popular ones are listed here. All carry a relatively high amount of protein, and each caters to an ideal balance of nutrition and good health both in physical terms and behaviorally. The snacks we've covered may be provisioned alongside any of these diets. These diets can be phased in during the later stages of puppyhood, but should only become full blown when the Coonhound reaches adulthood.

With all diets it's essential that you monitor closely both the state of your Coonhound's feces and also the overall weight. Try to keep exercise times quite rigid through the introductory days so that you can gradually work out precisely how much of each respective diet is perfect for the routine you and your Coonhound have worked out.

a) The Raw Diet

Enthusiastic about the dog's evolutionary history, some owners and even veterinarians will make an effort to recommend what the ancestor of all dogs - the wolf - ate as a diet. When wolves hunt they'll not only strip a carcass of skin, muscle and organs, but often opt to eat the bones too. The result is a high protein, low carb, high fiber diet which for all its flaws, sustained wolves for millennia until their cousin, the modern dog, was domesticated by ancient humans.

As with all diets it's imperative that you measure the dog's weight and apportion food using this as a guide. A useful marker to begin with is half a pound of food per 25 pounds of bodyweight daily.

Healthy Coonhounds range anywhere from 62 to 77lbs, and should therefore be fed around or just under 3lbs of raw (? "food") each day

 As a general guide, it's best to provide 80% raw muscle meat with fats, 10% organ tissues and 10% meaty bones. All of the material should be as fresh as possible. These figures are for an entire month: some days you can feed your dog liver, other days kidneys and meat, and so on. Much as wolves hunt a variety of quarry, so you should provide variance in the types and kind of meat you provide.

Freezing is an option, but meat which you freeze should be thawed and consumed within five days. If you wish to make the diet more organic and rounded, you can begin to introduce nutritious vegetables, most notably spinach and carrot.

How long the diet is maintained depends on your objective as the owner. Raw diets can be a kind of nutritious detox for dogs, a 'reset button' before you finally settle on something more moderate. Alternatively (and budget permitting) you might decide to make it a permanent arrangement.

Dogs on a raw diet do tend to display many signs of better health. Stools tend to be firmer, and so long as freshness is sustained, the dog's digestion will be natural and smooth. In the Coonhound's case, the short coat may take on an additional luster or shine, they may become overtly muscle-bound provided exercise continues strongly. Some dogs, including Coonhounds, can end up stocky despite their natural size, an appearance which appeals to some owners.

Since you'll be handling a lot more meat in your kitchen you must be sure to observe proper health and safety. If your counters have had raw meat upon them, they require thorough sanitation, as do your hands. Dogs are naturally resistant to bacterial diseases, but humans remain susceptible. As such, make precautions as you slice and dice your Coonhound's daily feed.

b) The Dehydrated Diet

At the other end of the canine dietary scale we've the dehydrated diet, which is longhand for 'dry diet'. Consisting of specialized dehydrated dog food, in recent years manufacturers have modified and re-modified formulas to reduce or remove the levels of grains and chemicals looked upon with increasing consternation by dog owners.

If you wish to keep your Coonhound exclusively on dried foods, be sure he's consuming more water to compensate. You'll likely find yourself refilling water bowls more often. Be sure also that your dog is well-hydrated prior to exercise. If you like spending lengthy periods exercising, having a well-watered dog is important. Coonhounds, especially those who are untrained, can even drink from unsanitary outside water sources such as ponds.

That said, dehydration is infrequent on this diet. Often owners will mix this and the raw diet. Kibble is used for foods which have been ground into shaped, fine pellets. The quality of this varies greatly, and I recommend asking vets for advice on a premium brand.

Expensive dog food will go much further to satisfying the essential vitamin and mineral requirements, whilst the carb and protein content will be of an overall better quality. Cheap filler, chemicals, and general sludge available under the 'value' or 'bargain' brands should be passed by. The phrase 'you get what you pay for' very much applies with dog food.

8) Choosing Some Good Bowls

You'll need two bowls for your Coonhound: one is for food and the other water. Depending on what you feed the dog the bowl can vary in terms of shape and size. If you want, you can use smaller bowls during the dog's puppyhood, buying new ones once your Coonhound approaches adulthood.

A wet diet merits a larger, concave shaped bowl so as to prevent mess and spillage in the eating area. Those feeding their dog a strictly dry diet needn't buy too large a dish, although both merit the proper materials.

Metallic, namely stainless steel, bowls tend to be the best. Your dog won't chew metals, and the durability of steel means you'll need no more than a few bowls throughout your Coonhound's life. Cleaning is likewise quite easy so long as it's done on a daily basis using your dishwasher or sink.

Ceramic bowls can act to be more decorative and presentable, some owners opting to have their dog's name printed upon the material. However they can become prone to chipping and cracks due to wear and tear. If you want such a bowl I recommend never to elevate it or leave it near ledges. Coonhounds can attack their food so voraciously that they might end up pushing the bowl far enough that it could fall.

Finally plastic, whilst cheap and available in many colors, is prone to the age old dog tendency of biting. Even a solid plastic bowl can attract a dog's teeth in the wrong sort of way: the weakness of the material has dogs commonly mistaking it as something to chew. Before long the bowl will be a mess of tooth marks and cracks, making it wise to avoid.

Chapter 11. Exercise, Play And Travel Concerns

Since by this point we've mentioned exercise in various contexts, its importance should be clear. Coonhounds thrive on exertion, they can walk for miles and never tire. Playing with a happy Coonhound is a workout in itself, and you shouldn't be surprised to find yourself out of breath at the end of play.

You don't buy a Coonhound if you don't want a dog that needs exercise. By extension this means that you should personally want to exercise. Getting a large dog, especially a scent hound with a hunting heritage, gives you plenty of excuses to get fit. Adulthood for a dog is about one year old, meaning that you can effectively keep your own fitness diary and increase the exertion month to month tied to your dog's growth.

Finding a happy medium between exercise, feeding and play is one of the most important undertakings of the first year of ownership. As your dog grows, different exercises and games can be attempted, as can longer walks. The great thing about adult Coonhounds is that the upper limit on walks is beyond what most humans can ever handle. If you can tire out your Coonhound on walks, you should probably think about running competitive marathons or taking up hiking. Nevertheless you should take care to set limits on exercise during the puppy stages, as well as paying attention to whether your dog is panting through dehydration.

The final portion of this chapter will inspect travel and the concerns you should address. This includes taking your dog between places, as well as finding places which will care for the dog when you'd like to take a holiday.

1) Exercising Your Coonhound

Whilst leaving a dog in your garden to roam might seem a quick fix, it's actually a great way to allow for bad habits to develop. Digging and generally tearing up your garden will take place even in a large yard, and your Coonhound will likely still want to blow off steam on reentering your house in the evening. This can mean unruliness, damage to furnishings and general rowdy misbehavior. All this still applies for a trained adult.

The backbone of any good exercise regimen is long walks. Couple this with a few episodes of rigorous play, ideal for the dog's age, and you'll be set. Given the quite hefty size and boundless energy of the Coonhound, at least an hour's worth of walking a day plus a further half an hour spent on energetic play should be aimed for.

If you've the time you can aim for more. However you should go much easier when the dog is still a young puppy. Initially you'll want to simply play and make short walks using a small leash. Starting when the dog is about six months of age you can start to work in the adult regimen.

An important rule of thumb is to always keep your Coonhound on a leash. Trained hunting hounds know to return to their owner after having tracked some game. A pet Coonhound however can sprint off so far and not think of returning, especially if it smells other creatures in the area.

A great way to exercise your dog is to drive a distance from home and go on an adventure.. This can mean daylong treks through tracks in the countryside, up hills and through woods. Such a time can be exciting, so long as your fitness permits it.

If you buy a long, retractable leash then you can safely play fetch with your Coonhound. Using open ground, you can have your dog bring a stick or Frisbee. Provided there are no other dogs around you can rub a little food or dog toothpaste on the object, have your dog sniff it and then throw it until he gets the idea.

2) Playtime!

In play, as with exercise, variety is important to observe. With walks this is often a matter of taking up a new route, letting your dog explore the new sights and smells. With play, however, there are a number of useful games and activities that will both excite and interest your Coonhound.

A general rule with play is to have frequent breaks. As well as allowing you to get your breath back, this can prevent the dog from getting out of control or overly frisky. Finish playing before you start to see your dog becoming bored or disinterested - the rule is to leave him wanting more.

As well as use of a Frisbee, you can play hide and seek by making use of the dog's intense sense of smell. Hiding toys that you've covered in meat around your garden or inside a bigger room of the house is a fun game to play. Given that the Coonhound was bred to find things using the nose this never fails to be entertaining.

From time to time you can combine this type of play with feeding time. Place your dog's usual portion of food in a bowl, and whilst he's inside, plant the pieces of food all around the yard. Not only will this prove a fun activity which rewards in itself, it can also serve to keep the dog's metabolism high. If you've a good sized garden it can also be a perfect pre-walk warm up.

Think of the popular game 'Go wild and freeze' as a dog themed take on a musical statues party game popular with kids. Start by dancing and running around excitedly, a behavior your Coonhound will quickly mimic. After a minute suddenly pause completely still and ask your dog to sit or stay. Then resume the game all over again, trying different commands in the process.

There are even simpler ways to mix things up. Using a garden hose at your dog can be a really fun game in itself. Don't spray directly at the dog - just let him chase and, if he likes, drink a bit of the water. This game can also serve to make your dog more amenable to water in general, making bath time that bit easier.

With the examples above you can see it's possible to combine training and feeding with exercise and play. Though your schedule should be quite rigid, the play itself should change. Rotate between perhaps half a dozen games, using different treats and training new commands to introduce some additional fresh variation. In this way play can serve a purpose and be enjoyable.

3) Travel Concerns

Whether you want to bring your dog on holiday, you're moving house or visiting a relative or friend, it is important to follow certain procedures to avoid difficulties on the road. If you happen to be staying in a hotel, it should allow pets - several large chain hotels at service stations will accommodate dogs.

Travelling via car tends to be easier with an adult than a puppy, given that adults can go for several hours without requiring bathroom breaks. With a puppy you ought to stop every couple of hours whilst keeping a ready supply of food and water in his crate. Depending on his age and your experience with his waste management, you can let him out of the crate to play and observe passing scenery.

If you're driving, be sure to have somebody holding the crate and keeping check on your dog. Large meals prior to the trip should be avoided, as dogs can end up with motion sickness and vomiting. On the road, stick purely to small protein-rich snacks. I often bring meatballs when taking my dog to the beach for a day. A few of these and plenty of water is enough to tide the dog over provided he's kept reasonably entertained.

For an adult, making sure they've gone to the toilet prior to your journey's start means less worry about the animal's comfort. Use of a sherpa (a bag with carry handles that the dog sits and sleeps in on long journeys) might be necessary depending on the journey's length. Road trips taking days make such things more necessary.

If you'll be away for some time, be sure to bring items that the dog is familiar with: his bowls, toys, blanket and so on. Let him play in the car, and allow him a view out of a window - often the passing sights will be of interest. You needn't sedate your dog with pills; a proper voice and friendly body language is the best medication your dog can have.

Make sure to tour him around your place of stay and aim to familiarize him throughout. After you've unpacked and settled in, take your dog on a walk around. Even if this happens to be around a bunch of parking lots at a service stop rather than something more luxurious, it will help assure the Coonhound that you're there for him and that things will be alright despite the new and strange surroundings.

Keep as close to your normal feeding schedule as you can and be sure you establish a place for him to toilet quickly. As with long walks, they'll be an overload of new smells which are bound to interest your Coonhound. Keep him on the leash when outside as you would at home and be sure you maintain your play and exercise schedule.

Lastly, you should try to enjoy yourself and refuse to be troubled on the trip. Coonhounds are very observant dogs, and will share in your worries should they be present. Sometimes this can manifest in barking or even aggression: at worst this can create something of a vicious cycle. Being casual and happy despite the stress that happens from time to time is important.

a) Restraints

Even if Coonhounds were small enough to fit in most laps, that wouldn't be a safe way to keep the dog on travels. More and more nowadays, countries and states are making it law to restrain your dog in a safe fashion. Buying a good harness for your dog is important for extended journeys. It's best to use these with adults given the issues with puppies and their bladder control and understanding of training.

A car harness should be highly secure. The market is unfortunately full of cheap restraint systems which are subject to no regulation by vehicle authorities as to their safety in crashes. One product that was recently tested as consistently safe in crash tests is the Clickit dog harness. As you'd expect it's a good deal more expensive than cheap dog seatbelts and harnesses, but unlike the myriad of cheap, untested items it will do the job of keeping the dog safe.

b) Exploring Options For Kennels

If, for whatever reason, you cannot or don't want to bring your Coonhound on travels and aren't able to leave him behind with a friend or relative as your dog sitter, you can look at kennels. Given the size and demanding nature of your Coonhound, however, you might find it more prudent to use a sitter hiring service.

Unless you feel certain that a kennel will suit your dog and that his high exercise requirements will be fulfilled, you can essentially book a holiday for your dog to stay with a family. These families are vetted as competent and able and you'll be interviewed by them to get a precise idea on the Coonhounds likes, dislikes and requirements. I will link some examples in the resources chapter.

If you do decide on kennels, be sure you tour one first, observing the conditions and happiness of the dogs present. Be sure to stress your Coonhound's requirements and see whether you're questioned about your dog's vaccination status. Checking for testimonials and the kennel's licensing status is also important.

In any event your Coonhound should be socialized and friendly with people. Although some professional sitters can cater otherwise, your dog should be both experienced and comfortable in a crate from his time as a puppy to avoid stress and discomfort in a kennel scenario.

c) Air Travel

If you've established that a given airline will permit travel, you must acquire the proper paperwork surrounding the dog's health. I do not recommend having a puppy travel by air. Not only must you have them fast for at least half a day which is bad enough in itself, but the experience can render your dog frightened and nervous for days. Crates are necessary from the moment you arrive at the airport to the time you've checked out of your destination airport. Food must be avoided, but water is fine in moderation to prevent your dog from being dehydrated.

Bear in mind that due to the noise and the motion of an aircraft, the experience will be stressful for any dog. In spite of their constitution, Coonhounds will find their time in the air difficult. Their weight and size will make them difficult to transport around the airport, although many airlines will help just after check-in. Expect your Coonhound to be stressed and very noisy in the bustle of your average terminal.

Chapter 12. Socializing

The best manners will get your dog invited to the best gatherings. Having a dog who is courteous and gracious to other people as well as other animals......? (this is not a complete sentence.) Socializing essentially means training your dog to get on well with those in the vicinity, with the exception of certain strangers.

Coonhounds tend to make reasonable guard dogs whilst still being courteous to those they know. Good social training will mean the mailman doesn't feel terrorized each time he makes his round, that you can invite people into your house for coffee or a chat without your dog kicking up a fuss. Well-trained Coonhounds can behave even in unusual circumstances, such as music playing during gatherings or meeting many new dogs in a local owner's group.

Socializing begins the very day you bring your new Coonhound home. Having each person in the house as well as other pets familiarize and interact with the dog is the beginning of his acquiring his graces. As with all training, socializing is a never-ending process, meaning that you'll need to reinforce what the dog has understood and assimilated whilst toning down the bad points.

In public, Coonhounds tend to carry a proud bearing and natural charisma. Through proper socializing you can take advantage of this manner, giving your dog the training necessary to sustain such charm and decorum wherever he is. This can be on walks around your area, on travels, when you have other people around as guests and so on. As heavily needful of exercise as Coonhound are, they can repay your efforts through behavior with others.

1) With Other Dogs, Pets and Animals

The first rule with a Coonhound puppy is repeated enforcement. Socializing is one thing you can do to apparent excess whilst still feeling comfortable Make sure that the pup grows to both respect and behave around any other pets you have at home.

In the initial days and weeks of ownership you'll want to give the dog a comparatively free rein in the house. If you've cats, make sure they can tolerate, play and generally get on well. In later life Coonhounds can become an active danger to your smaller pets, frightening them through chasing or even mauling them.

As such your first priority must be to render friendly your dog when it comes to other animals in the home. This is vital should you wish to introduce new pets in future. Your Coonhound's training must outweigh the hunting genes which resulted from centuries of intensive breeding.

Outside, your odds tend to dwindle the further you get from home. With supervision, your dog can get to know other dogs and pets in the neighborhood. Whilst forging a bond outside the home with these animals is likely optimistic, you can at least engender enough respect so that your neighbors won't need to fear.

On long walks the unfamiliar smells can overtake the Coonhound brain's impulses. A common phrase amongst the hunting enthusiasts is that the Coonhound brain turns off when the nose turns on. As such you should always keep the dog on a leash, perhaps even keeping him on a short leash on more distant treks. It can happen that the Coonhound catches the scent of some animal - possibly somebody's pet - and commences to chase them. Given the precision and bursts of speed the dog is capable of, it may even manage to injure or kill whatever it takes to chasing.

Despite this, training can act to inhibit such instincts. A Coonhound heavily used to other dogs and animals as pets will resist switching to chase mode. It is a matter of reinforcement and perseverance.

2) With Other People

Coonhounds can shine when dealing with other people. Often they'll assume a natural grace when guests arrive. Curious, but tending neither to hostility nor overt affection, a Coonhound of any breed can become a restrained and courteous part of your social life.

At first you'll be honing the dog's sociability in the home with those living inside it. Make sure that each member of the household treats the dog with kindness but doesn't get overexcited. Getting too active can end up switching your puppy to a play mindset, which can in turn affect any greeting or time with others.

The puppy months are brilliant at beginning these tendencies: a Coonhound in a loving home will grow up to be strong but sensitive, graceful but guarding. Being casual is the best way; during introductions, keeping your Coonhound on a leash is wise. If the dog does behave excitably simply ignore him and have guests do the same; with an absence of reaction your dog will soon revert to a less rambunctious manner so as to gain favor from you and your guests.

Slowly you can begin to introduce new people. Ideally before the Coonhound turns one, you should have introduced neighbors and some personal friends, initially one by one but later in pairs and groups. Observe your dog's conduct, and correct him with commands where appropriate. Your preference is important here; if you don't mind that your dog is affectionate and upfront, let them act such. If you'd rather your dog is very heedful of what you say when others are present, such as with tricks you've taught, then keep a bag of treats in your pocket ready for such displays.

Gradually you (should this be "he" i.e. the dog?) should build a tolerance and respect for others. If you know of other dog owners in your area, ask them if they'd mind if you joined them with your Coonhound. Keeping calm yourself can impact on the Coonhound's mind. When the phone rings or the postman calls, remain calm and scold your dog if necessary.

Conditioning your puppy to be social, or indeed to be trained and generally affable, depends on how you act and allocate your attention. Dogs crave and thrive upon attention, and will pay attention to your every move and change of tone in aid of gaining a perceived approval. Sometimes an absence of discipline can make your dog conclude that such and such a manner is acceptable, and this can lead to bad and even anti-social habits.

Eventually your casual, easy-going manner will hit home, leading to mimicry. As soon as your Coonhound gathers that you like him easy going and quiet when necessary, they'll be that way so long as you stay consistent. This manner can work right the way through socializing, all the way to a time when you can be assured of sensible behavior even when out meeting groups of other people.

3) Environmental Considerations

The place in which you live must be suitable for a Coonhound to grow and thrive as a well-adjusted dog. Bred for countryside use, the dog's ideal environment is rural, with a good sized property and garden to roam about in. Failing that, a large suburban home with good garden and parkland can suffice. Clean air, a variety of smells and sights and with enough of a human population present to ensure your dog develops a social attitude to most of what he encounters, are all important to your dog's sociability.

A good environment is vital simply because exercise and play - and the ground that requires for a large, energetic dog - is what underpins the finer points of your Coonhound's behavior. The ability to blow off the daily steam underpins a dog who can control himself, behave and cease with noise and fuss when the time calls for it.

Chapter 13. Poisonous Foods And Plants

There are a number of poisons your Coonhound can potentially consume. Not only are several household and garden plants dangerous to your dog, so too are several foods we humans enjoy regularly. Especially during the puppy months, dogs can gobble up things which smell interesting. Their tasting of things is almost an extension of the strong nose which governs many of their actions.

This can lead to unhealthy behaviors with worse consequences than the infamous consumption of other dog's excrement. Whilst that in itself is undesirable, it does not carry the danger which many items naturally toxic to dogs have. If poisoning does occur, it's important that you do not panic as this may only add stress to the discomfort your Coonhound already suffers. Following the steps in this chapter for prevention and treatment makes recovery all the more likelier.

We'll turn to and list all the major concerns. The importance of learning the appearance of wild plants is also beyond doubt: if walking your dog near fields and open country you can easily encounter poisons. Again, training comes into this: you can hold your dog's interest using treats, as well as conditioning him against consuming things on the road

The effects of poisoning are wide-ranging. In the best case scenario, often when your dog has ingested a stray piece of poison food, it will result in a relatively mild, short illness that you might not think to put down to poison. At worst however poison, can maim or kill a dog over a span of several pained and confused days.

If you want to keep the risk to your Coonhound as low as possible, invest some time in preventative measures. Rid your home of the poisonous substances below, and take care to cook with the foods mentioned infrequently or when the dog is out of the house.

116

Afterwards be sure to clean the kitchen well: even trace residues can render a hound ill.

1) Signs of Poisoning

Unless your dog ingests a very large amount of poison in a short time, which is an unlikely event in itself, there should be multiple signs you can readily observe. Coonhounds are blessed with strong bodies and organs, and will make sure you're aware of their state of being.

Differentiating a general illness or bug from poison is important, and can be accomplished by checking the animal's gums. As a rule the gums share their color with the dog's skin. If discoloration is spotted, you can test for it by applying pressure with a finger or thumb above one of the teeth. On releasing the pressure a change from white to pink indicates healthiness.

When your dog eliminates, discoloration of stools can denote poison present. If the excreta is watery this too makes poison more likely. Check your dog's temperature to see if it falls between the usual healthy range of 101 to 102.5 Fahrenheit.

Dizziness, staggering and general off-balance motion can also mean poison is present. Labored breathing or excess panting even after consuming water, can also denote poisoning

Before calling the vet be sure you've written down your observations. Check around your house for any disturbed chemicals. Be certain that none of the foods you have in the kitchen dangerous to dogs could have been consumed.

With Coonhounds a contaminated rodent that has been caught can also be the culprit. Some fungi and mushrooms which often mature around September can emerge in gardens and be eaten. In any case below are listed the commoner plants and foods which can cause poisoning.

2) Poisonous Foods

Often when a dog observes his masters eating and enjoying something, he'd like to join in. The Coonhound nose is no deterrent to poisons; if something smells interesting and looks edible, the dog will eat it. If he sees you eating it first, all the more so.

Note that you needn't stop consuming what's listed here. Simple safe procedure and cleaning, as well as memorizing and cautioning everyone in the home about these poisonous foods means exclusion needn't be necessary

Avocados became popular in the West from the 1970s onwards. One of the best sources of fats from a fruit, they are popular with seafood, in sandwiches or eaten alone with salt. Take care with the fruit, skin and leaves - all are poisonous to dogs.

Uncooked bread dough is likewise dangerous. The live yeast present can expand inside your dog's system, resulting in organ damage. It produces alcohols which are highly poisonous to your dog. If you happen to enjoy home baking, take extra caution when preparing loaves or other baking products.

Chocolate is the commonest food a dog is poisoned by. A naive child can easily give it a little. Chemicals called metyhlxanthines within chocolate are very dangerous to dogs, causing a myriad of symptoms such as extreme thirst, irregular heartbeat, a temperature and aggression. The darker the chocolate is, the more damage it can do.

Alcohol (ethanol) has a far greater sensitivity with dogs. Even a spillage lapped up can lead to dangerous vomiting and intoxication. Beer, wine and dairy cocktails can all appeal to a dog, and should be consumed with care if your dog is around. If you happen to engage in home brewing, bear in mind that both hops and yeasts are poisonous too.

Grapes and raisins can cause kidney trouble, although some dogs can consume them harmlessly. If enough are eaten, vomiting can ensue, followed by a disinterest in food and drink. If untreated, death from kidney failure can ensue within 72 to 96 hours.

Garlic and onions are toxic and shouldn't be given to dogs. This includes powdered forms, which can be even more dangerous due to concentration of certain chemicals.

Macadamia nuts rarely threaten a dog's life but can render them uncomfortable for up to two days.

Xylitol is an increasingly commoner sweetener seen in certain candies and chewing gums. Dogs can experience drastic drops in blood sugar from even a moderate amount of this substance, and heavy consumption can mean liver failure.

Anything moldy should be avoided. If you've a compost heap in the garden, be sure to keep it fenced off from your dog, who may take to eating any rotting fruit or other decomposing matter you place there. The bacteria can pose a high threat to dogs. Be sure also to remove anything moldy from the kitchen.

3) Poisonous Household Plants

I will list here the commoner plants seen in gardens and potted in households. The effects vary but often include skin rashes, diarrhea, vomiting and general pain and discomfort, with repeated ingestion leading to serious illness. As a rule you should remove these plants from your home and garden if present. Fallen leaves and flowers can easily be eaten by your dog.

Please note that **these lists are not complete**: the number of plants poisonous to dogs includes further, but rarer species. Included here are the commoner ones:

Asparagus Fern (berries only)	Aloe Vera
Amaryllis	Azalea/Rhododendron
Bird of Paradise	Buttercups
Carnations	Caladium
Castor Beans	Chrysanthemum
Corn Plants	Cyclamen

Daffodils	Dieffenbachia
Elephant Ears	Hostas
Horse Chestnut	Ivy
Mistletoe (berries only)	Morning Glory (including seeds)
Nicotiana (tobacco plant)	Pothos
Rhubarb (leaves only)	Rosary Pea (seeds only)
Tomato plants	Tulips
Yew (bark and leaves)	

4) Grasses and Wild Plants

To a large extent there is overlap between wild plants and trees and those you'll see in parks and landscaped gardens. In some cases well-tended wildflowers can be included in these places. If you plan on taking the dog or whole family to botanic gardens, be sure to keep your dog under close observation. Smelling the plants is okay, but sampling them can be dangerous:

Arrowgrasses	Baneberries
Box shrubs	Buckeye
Chinaberry tree	Cowbane
Corn cookie	Common privets
Cowslip	Daphne
Delphinium	Elderberry tree
False flax	Fan weed
Field peppergrass	Foxglove
Hyacinth	Iris
Jatropha	Jerusalem Cherry

Jimsonweed	Laburnum
Larkspur	Laurels
Lupines	Mayapple
Milk vetch	Monkshood
Moonseed	Mustards (seeds only)
Nightshade	Oleander
Pokeweed	Poison hemlock
Potatoes (shoots and sprouts)	Rattle box
Skunk cabbage	Smartweeds
Snow-on-the-mountain	Sorgham grass
Star of Bethlehem	Velvet grass
Wild radishes (seeds)	Woody aster
Yellow pine flax	

5) Removing Poisons From Your Home

Keeping your home poison-free is as much about prevention as it is removal. You should be on your guard when you decide to fix up your garden. Be sure to pick plants which aren't poisonous.

Make sure that you store all detergents and household cleaners in a high cupboard. Similarly if you've a garage, store any oils, antifreeze, WD40 and other chemicals safely away. Furniture polish, bleaches, insecticides and bug sprays and any spray-on cleaners for the car, kitchen or elsewhere should all be kept out of reach.

As has been noted, be sure that your kitchen is cleaned and tidied. Be sure to store away anything poisonous. If you're hosting friends for drinks, be sure to tell them to take care; spilt alcohol can do huge harm to your dog.

If your home is unfortunate enough to become infested, requiring a pest control firm or thorough spraying, be sure to inquire with those cleaning that the fumigation will not leave traces of poison in the atmosphere dangerous to pets. If you find a reputable firm, usually they'll provide guarantees to this end.

Medications, be they painkillers, contraceptives or even vitamin and mineral supplements can result in harm for your dog. Be sure to pick up and dispose of any tablets you drop, and keep your medicines safely stored away. There are medications aimed at pets, but be sure to talk with the vet before giving your Coonhound any, to avoid health complications.

Coonhounds are known for their noisiness. If you feel a neighbor is unhappy with the barking and baying the breed is known for, try to work it out. Occasionally people in the neighborhood can become resentful and intentionally leave poisons at or near your gate or property entrance for your dog to consume. Minimize this risk with friendliness and discussion.

6) Animal Poison Control Centre (APCC)

If you believe your Coonhound has ingested poisons, you can call your vet with details or opt to call specialists in the form of charitable bodies. Unlike most vets, these places operate 24 hours a day offering consultations.

It is possible that you'll be charged a fee for this service, however you can ask the operator about this at the start of your call.

You can read up on this at:

http://www.aspca.org/pet-care/animal-poison-control

The hotline number is (888) 426-4435.

Chapter 14. Caring For The Ageing Coonhound

Helping a Coonhound through old age is an effort which should be looked upon as a reward for your dog's years as a family member. Coonhounds will often navigate life with vigor, making old age all the more stark as their mobility and senses begin to suffer.

At this point it is likely you've owned the dog for years, have long had a comfortable schedule in place, and have all sorts of happy memories of the time you spent together. It's likely your Coonhound has shared in good times and bad, has been both a comfort and a source of stress, but through everything has become treasured in your household.

Generally there is only minor variation in lifespan between the Coonhound breeds. Assuming no major illnesses or traumas occur, the dog can expect to live for perhaps 12 to 14 years. As with many breeds, anomalies can happen - Coonhounds living 18 years or more isn't unheard of. Given the energy and vigor for which they are renowned, age can render a Coonhound inactive. The first thing you will notice is a slow decrease in time spent exercising.

Dealing with the advancement of age is a gradual process. Old age for a Coonhound arguably begins at about age 8, meaning that potentially a third or more of your dog's life will involve the adjustments I'll talk about here. We'll move through the physical and psychological sides of aging, to topics such as euthanasia and bereavement. Finally, I'll finish up with a personally written poem that I hope will offer some comfort.

1) Things To Be Aware Of

As in humans, aging is gradual. Although this chapter lists all kinds of things, it is very likely they'll have to be dealt with a bit at a time. Aging of dogs is as much an enduring mystery as aging in humans. Much as our digestion slows with age, so too does a dog's. White hairs, changes in skin quality, muscle and bone weakness are all facts of life for the aged dog.

Unlike many humans, dogs require strong adjustments in diet throughout old age. Often this can mean dog foods, dry or otherwise, with certain vitamins heightened in the interest of your dog retaining as much function as possible. Many raw diet enthusiasts claim the high protein levels can ensure vigor is maintained even into old age.

Regardless of your belief and dietary regime, you should expect to see a reduction in appetite as your dog becomes elderly. Dental problems are frequent even if you've kept up a lifelong, even daily, tooth brushing schedule. The teeth naturally become more susceptible and weaker, often necessitating a diet of softer, less chewy foods worked into the diet.

Although blessed with good coping of temperature and weather changes in spite of their short coats, an older Coonhound will start to falter in their tolerance of rain and may start shivering before you can get home or back to the car. Buying a water proof dog Macintosh jacket or cloth and fabric jacket can ward off such sensitivities for a time. Eventually however you must shorten your walks so as not to strain or pressure the Coonhound.

Most importantly you should be in close touch with your vet through this time, making check-ups every few months. Your vet will be able to confer treatment for general complaints like fleas in a manner sensitive to your Coonhound's age. Eventually they'll might offer you a full geriatric care program in the interest of preserving health for as long as possible.

a) Physiological Changes

Many of the bodily changes your Coonhound goes to can be summed up in the catch-all term 'slowing down'. Loss of vigor in play and exercise is gradual, but noticeable in the Coonhound. Even if you're doing your utmost to keep the dog interested, his mind may wander and his enthusiasm wane. Where he used to bound up and down stairs, he may now hesitate or do so awkwardly.

In the worst case your Coonhound will lose the ability to run and have a lameness in his walk. This can mean osteoarthritis, a common ailment in old dogs, has happened. There are varying degrees of severity, meaning that it's possible to simply shorten your play and exercise regime. Consultation with your vet including x-rays can clue you in.

Deafness will often occur to an aging dog. In some cases it can be sudden, but sometimes infections, abscesses or even certain parasites can induce loss of hearing. If your Coonhound does become deaf or hard of hearing, be sure to walk them further from dangers such as passing traffic.

The proud, muscular bearing all Coonhounds possess will start to lessen in old age. Although your dog is unlikely to look skinny, the stockiness he was known for will likely diminish. If it strikes you that the atrophy has struck certain body parts heavily, talk to your vet as this can be a sign of illness rather than natural aging.

A graying of the muzzle and face is natural. Sometimes even a young dog can suffer this change in appearance prematurely. Coonhounds will suffer a change in eye color too: aged dogs' eyes often assume a bluish, cloudy texture. Contrary to popular belief this needn't be the start of cataracts which are white and opaque. Once again, veterinary consultation will set things straight.

Your dog's temperament will generally mellow with old age. Whilst a Coonhound never gives up the enthusiasm for barking they are renowned for, an old dog will tend to tone down such behavior. This is perfectly normal and healthy.

However as time goes on it is possible the canine equivalent of dementia and Alzheimer's disease will emerge. This often entails your dog being up at all hours, being consistently inattentive, as well as confused and disorientated, Showing strange behaviors and habits, such as staring straight ahead, or persistently dull in obeying commands or even listening at all.

Fortunately treatment, often with drugs closely related to those used in humans, have been shown to be effective. Consulting with your vet if you believe your dog is developing dementia could well restore his abilities for a long time.

With Coonhounds it is also possible for depression to strike, especially when your dog can no longer exercise or play as he could. This can be alleviated by simply taking your dog for a ride, and playing for as long as possible without discomfort developing. Coonhounds thrive on activity, but have enough intelligence and adaptability to come to terms with the shortcomings of age. A gentle and forgiving attitude is often best, letting your dog know that despite his difficulties and slower nature you still value and care for him.

Often a dog can become depressed due to pain which you mightn't realize was happening. This can be the case if for instance, arthritis occurs in the spine or neck, thereby being subtler than if it were to affect the legs. A visit to the vet can establish the existence of pain, which can be treated through medications.

b) Geriatric Dogs

Agedness in Coonhounds carries a whole new set of pitfalls and things to observe. On the one hand, the reduction in enthusiasm, risk-taking and general activity will make ingestion of strange things or risks of escape much reduced.

On the other hand, however, you must keep an eye on your dog's consumption of food and overall weight. At this stage in life, every bit of excess weight can mean added strain on joints. A healthy old Coonhound should be slim but not gaunt. A sudden reduction in weight may indicate internal issues, as can excessive thirst. Persistent coughing can indicate respiratory issues, as can sudden onset of disorientation, bad breath, or sudden appearance of lumps on the body which can be either benign growths or cancerous tumors.

Cross training - use of signals to signify commands - can pay dividends at this stage in the dog's life. If deafness does occur, you'll still be able to command your dog as needed. Given that hygiene and cleaning are more important than ever for the aging dog, it can make grooming much easier.

Bear in mind also the diminished temperature control many old dogs have. This can lead to pneumonia, itself a dangerous and frequent cause of death in older humans. As with people, it can be difficult to provide enough insulation and care for the ailment to subside. The same is the case for excess heat. Dehydration, heatstroke and other serious ailments can affect an older dog, who ideally, should stay in a cool, shaded place in summertime.

Veterinarians will often offer an all-round care package for dogs over a certain age. Given that cancer affects over half of all dogs over age ten, signing up to such an offer means you'll be informed and able to choose whether your dog should undergo surgery or not. Remember that veterinary science is advancing all the time, meaning that your dog can keep a quality of life for longer.

c) Adjusting Bathroom Schedules

Much as puppies suffer from poor control over their bladder, so too do older dogs. You should gradually adjust their housetraining schedule and feeding times to cope with any sudden or gradual loss of control. Help such as ramps can assist your dog in navigating outside. Although a Coonhound's size prohibits all but the largest of outdoor dog playpens, such a pen might be a consideration with age so long as the climate and weather permit.

Urinary tract infections and various diseases and maladies affecting the digestion can also aggravate the situation. Testing for such ailments, for instance Cushings disease or diabetes, can be accomplished via testing.

If you've harder floors it can be advisable to lay down some disposable cheap throw rugs to avoid slippage on urine. If urination is especially frequent and there is certainly no issue present other than old age, this may prove a good solution. In the final stages of your dog's life, physically carrying the dog out to his longtime elimination spots might well be the most straightforward thing to do.

d) Ensuring Comfort

Your dog's comfort should gradually become a greater priority as old age advances. Without doubt your Coonhound will be spending more time in the home, meaning that you should make some modifications. If arthritis or other maladies related to the joints are an issue, increased padding on your dog's bed can help.

Medications often become a huge part of keeping your dog comfortable and happy. These can act to reduce pain, discomfort or, in the case of dementia, restore a presence of mind. Furthermore the side effect profile of many modern meds is limited, meaning they're a credible way to assure your dog maintains comfort.

Often plenty of love and affection can be more meaningful than pillows and blankets. Given that your dog will be inside the house more, spend time simply sitting and petting him in a casual manner. Genuine affection can act to relax your Coonhound, appealing to the sensitive side he no doubt has.

2) Old Age Checklist

I'll now list each major area of concern for the aged dog, and how best to address it.

a) Frequent Check-ups

A rule of thumb with old dogs is to increase the frequency at which you visit the vet. Although the precise frequency will depend on what your vet recommends and what perennial issues your Coonhound has, by reaching old age, generally 4 to 6 times a year is a good ballpark figure.

Although this increased frequency will entail higher expense, sometimes veterinarians will offer a reasonable package deal. Preventative measures can also serve to prolong your dog's life and quality of life

b) No Vigorous Play and Gentler Exercise

Walks should be gradually shortened in keeping with your impressions of the Coonhound's comfort. Exercise should never be stopped entirely unless your dog is completely unable to undertake it. Instruct members of the household to treat your dog gently and not be disappointed should the hound be disinterested in playing.

Sometimes altering the pace of your walk, allowing your dog to take breaks, can serve to maintain a decent length over time. Play, however, should be markedly more easy going. Sudden excitement tends not to work well with older dogs, but gentle games of fetch or hiding food around the garden can still act to keep your dog happy.

c) Ensuring Quality Food

Often older dogs must eat dog food specifically aimed at seniors. Given the increased hydration needs and fragility of the teeth, a soft, wet dog food can prove favorable. Should you wish to maintain a raw diet high in proteins, opt for softer meat. Eventually, however, it can be necessary to supplement a mostly meat diet with other foods to tend to vitamin and mineral deficiencies common in the older dog.

Often old dogs can become reluctant to eat. This can be true of Coonhounds despite their voracious eating habits. Often they'll smell changes in the food, and be quite wary for a time. Importantly you shouldn't be impatient or angry at this perceived choosiness, and should instead try varying both meal times and the exact contents of your dog's meals.

d) Keeping Your Dog Clean and Parasite-free

An aged Coonhound will lose the natural sheen a well looked after coat has. This is not in itself a problem and indicates nothing more than natural aging. Despite such a loss in luster, you should continue tending to your dog in much the usual way. Grooming should, however, be gentle: do not scrub at the coat vigorously as this can cause hair loss or even pain to your dog. As with most everything else, it's a matter of finding balance between vigor in washing and keeping your pet comforted.

Dealing with parasites is another reason for regular vet visits. Any aging dog will be more vulnerable to the various negative effects different parasites and worms bring. Effects leading on from infestation can be much more serious, potentially leading to complications along the line. For this reason, regular observations of symptoms should be made.

e) Warmth

Warmth, both steady and consistent, is vital for an aged dog's well-being. Extra blankets, a dog coat, and adjusting the place in which he sleeps to a warmer or cooler part of the home should be undertaken when your dog reaches old age.

Some experimentation is required so that you can discover your dog's ideal temperature. Coonhounds are bred to be hardy in this area, therefore your dog might enjoy a relative lack of sensitivity of temperature. Nevertheless you should keep a close eye for discomfort; repeated instances where the ambient temperature is outside your pet's comfort zone can lead to health complications.

f) Hydration

An unfortunate paradox of old age is both the sustained need for water and a general loss of control of bladder function. Despite a fall in activity, you'll still need to hydrate your Coonhound regularly. A Coonhound of 60lbs who is no longer exercising should consume about 4 to 5 bowls of water a day alongside some well-hydrated food. This may rise even in marginally warmer weather due to sensitivity; be prepared for change.

Sometimes when an old dog is ill, the act of drinking water or eating can be difficult due to pain or disinterest. Encourage your dog to drink by offering him some water to lick on your fingers; this will cause him to associate it with you, his master. Always be sure that the water is regularly freshened, and think about making more soups and stews in lieu of plain water.

3) What Is Euthanasia?

Euthanasia is a term referring to intentionally and humanely ending a life through artificial means. With dogs this can mean undergoing either one or two injections at the vets which will induce a painless death usually within a minute.

Sometimes vets will make one injection to tranquilize the dog, allowing you to say goodbye on your own terms and in good time, before a second injection is administered which will put the dog permanently to rest.

Often your vet will offer euthanasia once it is clear to them professionally that your dog is unable to continue life without substantial or extreme pain and discomfort on a near-continuous basis. Such circumstances can be due to terminal illness such as cancer, as well as dangerous and contagious illnesses such as rabies. Highly aggressive dogs may also be euthanized.

Tragically, many animals are put to sleep simply because of overpopulation in shelters. Coonhounds are frequently seen in shelters and puppies or young adults may meet this fate if adoption does not occur.

Sometimes you can ask your vet to perform the procedure at home. Given their professional capacity in tending to farm animals, this practice is commoner in rural vets. If you believe your dog would be too uncomfortable to even make the trip to the veterinary center, you may be able to arrange an appointment for this to happen. Prior to the day, you can make arrangements for cremation and start to prepare a gravesite at your home.

If you wish to let your dog go at the vets, make sure that you constantly make efforts to comfort and reassure the dog. Stroke and talk to him tenderly. Don't suppress your emotions after your Coonhound's departure. Your vet has seen these things many times before and is well-equipped to comfort you in your grief.

4) Helping Your Dog As The End Nears

Whether you choose to end your dog's life with the assistance of your vet, or whether your dog departs naturally in your home, it's helpful to make preparation for your dog's comfort. Often the circumstances of the departure can affect your grieving process.

Before the pain or trials of old age become too much for the dog, you can take a holiday or journey together. Letting your dog experience something new on a final adventure can be a reminder of why you took on the responsibility of ownership in the first place. If a holiday is relaxed and laid back, both you and your dog will head home with happy memories.

If you believe your dog will expire naturally, try to have him lay down on a blanket close to the fire. If he's unable to move, position his head upon a pillow and partly cover his body with the quilt. Prepare a final meal; this needn't be large or elaborate - often some meat will do - but should be your Coonhound's favorite.

As your dog is laying there, be sure to talk to him softly. You can even sing a song if your dog enjoys that. Assure him that things will be fine, and that he'll begin a new journey. You and your family can each pet and stroke your dog in turn, before you give him a final hug.

Although tears may come, remember that you should be glad that you got to spend years of happiness together. Recall the good times you had, the people he gave joy to, the times of frustration and joy and excitement and relaxation.

5) The Grieving Process

Grief for your deceased Coonhound, or any deceased pet, shares much in common with what you'd feel for a departed individual. Since there's no definitive timeframe for grief, you may feel such a gap in your life for a long time before you fully come to terms with the death.

Accepting the loss is important. Realizing that your Coonhound has departed for good is a positive thing. Discuss your memories with friends and family, talk about his habits and oddities and memorable moments. Although sadness is a natural part of the grieving process, fond remembrance can be too. Loneliness can be relieved through reliving the times you enjoyed with your departed pet.

Try not to feel guilty or inadequate or ashamed, or let anyone tell you how to feel. Arguing about your feelings won't help matters. A negative attitude to the loss can prolong your sadness, and will curtail perspective on the abundance of positives your dog brought to life. However such emotions can be, to an extent, unavoidable.

Despite the sadness, you should make effort to maintain a healthy sleeping and waking cycle, eat right, and exercise. Getting into a routine without your pet can make the grief pass easier.

Often dedicating a memorial to your dog can be a good way for you to honor your pet's legacy. If you've children present, you can consider the passing to be an opportunity for them to learn about death. An upfront, honest discussion about it without euphemisms or stories can help young members of your family come to terms with future loss.

Finally, in the long run you can think about getting a new dog or pet generally. If you've gotten through grief with a positive outlook, that your life and the life of your dog was one of mutual benefit and happiness, you might start to think about adopting or buying another dog so that your skills and experience can help another dog live a happy, fulfilling life.

6) Making A Memorial

Buying or making a grave for your dog is a worthwhile way in which to honor his contribution to your life. Many owners opt for a simple plaque or stone, choosing to decorate it only sparsely. Despite this there are a variety of more elaborate options available.

If you seek a simple headstone or simply a shaped stone to place in your garden, there are many companies who will craft such things. Often you can request custom eulogies together with your dog's name to be engraved upon the rock.

If you had your dog cremated it is also possible to store their ashes in an urn. A small indoor memorial can be created perhaps near where your pet slept. You can be inventive with floral displays. A friend of mine even had his old dog's bowls welded to his dog's grave site.

It's often good to place your dog's grave near a bench or sitting area in your back yard. As you sit out there during a warm afternoon or evening, you'll might find yourself pleasantly reminiscing about your dog.

Burial is something which is usually undertaken after your dog passes away at home. It is of course optional: there are pet funeral homes who will collect the body and cremate it. Some of these companies even offer pet funerals, which can be a great way to bring family, friends and neighbors together in commemoration of your dog's life.

7) A poem To Remember

One week old, truth be told

I cannot hear or see

Ten weeks old, my siblings sold

A person collected me

Six months now, I run and howl

I feel loved all the while

Two years passed, I'm sprinting fast

Smells and sights for miles

Five years gone, my bones are strong

Master makes food and words for me

Twelve years young, or am I more?

My memory is not so keen

Old, tired and sleepy I close my eyes

Master's smile, the last thing I'd seen

Chapter 15. Shelters

Some of the resources listed here are not specific to Coonhounds. However, in the case of shelters, a phone call to inquire as to the breeds present can yield results.

Despite their heritage as a desired and well-bred hunting dog, the Coonhound can find themselves in shelters with a surprising frequency. Across certain areas they aren't desired much outside of hunting circles. Accidental litters especially can and have led to busy adoption schedules by volunteer groups.

If you're in the position to drive a good distance you can easily employ the genuine good will and compassion of many individuals involved in finding Coonhounds both puppy and adult new homes. As with breeders, those in charge will spell out the application process clearly and will be sure to query you to the point where becoming an owner of a Coonhound feels like trying for a job. In a way, given the nature of the dog, it is one!

Colorado area - http://www.coloradocoonhounds.4t.com/

Petfinder - website which allows for searching for specific dogs in a database: http://www.petfinder.com

Shelter exchange - lists regional and local shelters across the USA - http://www.shelterexchange.org

Charleston Pet Connect - regional website listing shelters and other resources specific to Southern U.S. states: http://www.charlestonpetconnect.com/

Adopt a Pet - Another website which lists registered rescues and shelters including those specific to Coonhounds: http://www.adoptapet.com/

Chapter 16. Additional Resources

In addition to the list of forums and breeders I (mentioned?) earlier, here are some other websites and blogs dedicated wholly to Coonhounds and how great they are, followed by a few websites specific to certain concerns, including that of poison control.

This list includes clubs as well as enthusiast websites which invite participation: you can post pictures and share joy with other, like-minded people. The added perk in talking about Coonhound ownership is that it might lead others to take on one themselves.

Further pages include links to more specific websites; breeding authorities, pet supply stores, rescue centers and memorials respectively.

Coonhound Companions is a group of Coonhound enthusiasts from all around the USA. Dedicated to spreading the word about how Coonhounds make great pets as well as hunting hounds, the website began in 2010 and has since attracted sponsorship and a devoted following: http://www.coonhoundcompanions.com/

Maddie the Coonhound - a cute website by a passionate Coonhound owner. Features stories and galleries of the titular Coonhound and her antics: http://www.maddieonthings.com/

AKC Coonhounds - though focused on hunting, this website has a large community of dedicated Coonhound owners and has plenty of general information and a forum: http://www.akccoonhounds.org/

Australian Dog Forum - a wide-ranging forum with occasional discussion of scent hounds and Coonhounds: http://www.australiandogforum.net

Pet Forums - British forum inviting discussion and sharing of anything at all dog related: http://www.petforums.co.uk/

1) Breeder Information, Registry Authorities

Australia, New South Wales registry

http://www.dogsnsw.org.au/breeding/how-to-become-a-breeder.html

New Zealand Kennel Club, includes membership, rules and info

http://www.nzkc.org.nz/

Canadian Kennel Club, includes membership and rules

http://www.ckc.ca/

American Kennel Club, membership, rules and resources included

https://www.akc.org/

British dog breeding licensure rules for commercial breeders

https://www.gov.uk/dog-breeding-licence-england-scotland-wales

2) Rescue Centers

(Note: many more area-specific Coonhound websites exist)

For Black and Tan Coonhounds nationwide

http://www.coonhoundrescue.com/

Northeast Coonhound Rescue, all breeds

(New England area, USA) http://necoonhoundrescue.org/

Carolina Coonhound Rescue, all breeds

http://www.carolinacoonhoundrescue.com/

Gentle Jake's Coonhound Rescue

(Canada) http://www.coonhoundrescue.ca/

3) Equipment And Supply Outlets

(Note: these are just a few suggestions. There are many stores online competing in the pet supply market. Even popular websites like Amazon now have reputed sellers with numerous dog products on their stores. Shop around!)

PetSmart - many different accessories & products (USA & Canada)

http://www.petsmart.com/

Pet Planet - popular British store, wide-ranging products on offer

http://www.petplanet.co.uk/

Mammoth Pet Supplies - Australian pet store, huge range

http://www.mammothpetsupplies.com.au/

Pet Post - New Zealand premier outlet for dog and pet supplies

http://www.petpost.co.nz/

4) Memorials

Peternity - offers urns, graves & memorial markers (USA & Canada)

http://www.peternity.com

Pet Memorials - wide range of memorial supplies tailor-made (UK)

http://www.pet-memorials.co.uk/

Pet Heaven Memorials - engraving, headstone, urns (Australia)

http://www.petheavenmemorials.com.au/

Pet Memories - memorials, urns (New Zealand)

http://www.petmemories.co.nz

CPSIA information can be obtained
at www.ICGtesting.com
Printed in the USA
BVHW04s2305280618
520323BV00010B/61/P